ANTICS & ANECDOTES

By Pablo Marchant

THE CHAIN GANG

Antics and Anecdotes

Photographs: Pablo Marchant
Formatting: Honesty Press
ISBN: 978-17396495-8-6 (Hardcover)
First edition: July 2024

10 9 8 7 6 5 4 3 2 1

Introduction

I was born to English parents and raised in a jungle, in a country called Paraguay in South America. My primitive lifestyle and schooling was not more than 14 years and frequently interrupted due to lack of teachers and illness.

While my elder siblings were working with machinery etc. I was drawn into this exciting life of repair, driving tractors and working with electrics at a very early stage in my school life, up to and until the age of 16, that is when I moved to England.

I was 16 years of age and 6 ft 1" tall. My parents wanted me to carry on with my schooling. I was assessed to enter a class of 12-year-olds. I made it quite clear that this was not what I was going to do. I found employment relatively easy to get in the early 1960 and I never looked back.

I was drawn into the field of mechanical and electrical work especially diagnosing and repairing. I was self-taught and at times had to work alongside academics, I found them at times very difficult to understand as I had to ask questions. Many times, their diagnosis clashed with mine. Yet I did recognise them for achieving a recognised certificate.

Ian, my very good friend, knew about me trying to write stories about my work experiences, and offered to take me to a small English class. Knowing full well of my upbringing and that I had no English language skills behind me.

He encouraged me just to go and listen, nothing more. On the first visit and the following 2 or 3 weeks I had anxiety big time my brain was screaming; "What the hell am I doing here? I don't understand the spelling let alone the grammar; I need to get out of here!"

But thinking back, what kept me going was a strong desire to put this down on paper, as what I experienced in my working life environment was unbelievable.

A few weeks passed and I found myself sort of slotted into a very friendly group, and homely feeling. Everybody gave me however small encouragement to continue.

This is run informally and with compassion by a bright young English Writing Graduate (MA).

We (6 of us) sitting around the table was very daunting for me. Slowly! I progressed, as each week they gave valuable advice and constructive criticism to my short stories.

Part 1:

Fire College

I was the first employed by the Home Office as fire ground crew at the New Fire Service Technical College at Moreton-in-Marsh in1969.

A Senior Fire Officer who organised three practical courses saw me standing around (or other people would call it loitering) in a long corridor amongst other old buildings and asked me what my job was. I told him.

"Come with me," he said.

I didn't know if I should. We entered his office. He sat down and told me to take a chair. Very well mannered, he told me that I was seconded to his department. I didn't know if this was true or not. He made it clear that I should go and get a vehicle from the transport department (wherever that was?) then report back to him. He would arrange all by phone.

My job or duties grew by the day, extremely interesting and meant a lot of driving as this place was an ex-RAF base. The courses consisted of intakes every 3 weeks, 4 weeks and 11 months.

I was trained in servicing breathing apparatus and all necessary equipment used by the three courses. Plus all equipment used by students in class rooms etc.

ME AND A SAFETY OFFICER

Consequences

I was the first employee in the roll of fire ground crew. The commanding officer of the new teaching block made a job vacant for me and told the Home Office Staff and Secretary that I was now in his teaching block.

Three types of courses were as follows: Road Accident (a 3-week course running consecutively). Station Officer (a 4-week course running consecutively). APC (Accelerated Promotion Course). This was a full 11-month long course.

In due course, after training and instruction, I was put in charge of all fire fitting apparatus. This included all mechanical, breathing apparatus, lifting tackle etc. All of this equipment was used for training purposes.

I had to make certain that all classrooms were adequately supplied with the relevant equipment, such as overhead projectors, 16mm projectors, and a contraption called an epidiascope (which solely projected images of opaque objects) and that students had sufficient Stationery to carry out their homework.

Every 3rd and 4th week, the Road Accident and Station Officer course, on their last training week, one of the students of each course would book a local pub in the neighbourhood. Either the whole pub or the room of the pub, this would be off-limits to the public, and these officers would organise their entertainment. I hasten to add all the entertainment was completely surprising to me. Now, I was thrown into the male quagmire; they organised all sorts, some courses had strippers, some hardcore blue movies, (embarrassing the first-time round!). It was a huge learning curve of how young officers of whom some are married and have families behaved in a gang like culture with huge volume alcohol mixed in. I got anesthetised to this behaviour and turned this to my advantage; it gave me the opportunity to do tasting of specialist beers which was wonderful. The food: usually chicken in the basket, was free of charge to me. This went on for the remainder of my stay at the College (18 months or so).

Most Wednesdays I was commandeered to take a group of officers to Cheltenham Town Hall where dances etc were held. On this particular Wednesday the "APC" (Accelerated Promotional Course) was taken to Cheltenham, and I collected them at around 22:30 and brought them back to their dormitory. A 3-story apartment block.

I put the vehicle back in the hangar and walked back to their dormitories (as I was invited) where I had some bottles of beer waiting. On entering the top corridor, there was a lot of rapid banging against the wall, plus a hell of a lot of shouting and general hoo-hah.

Most of the officers were out of their bedsit and milling about in the corridor. I made for the far end of the corridor. Negotiating officers were wondering about with bottles of beer and shouting, yelling. I got to the bedsit which was occupied by a Cheltenham officer. On entering, I commented about the racket. A few minutes or so later, amongst the racket, I heard a female laughing, screaming and yelling out loud: "Never mind me yelling, let me have it!"

That was scary, as I had no idea that there was a woman in the quarters. I knew now what that banging was, this officer was being ridden well and truly by this woman.

This officer had a plastered leg and was on 2 crutches due to accident some weeks back. I had to chauffeur him around. That's how I got to know him. His home was northeast of England. Very occasionally he went home weekends, as it would take him fifteen hours door to door one way. He was a ladies' man, always late to be picked up from the dances. On this occasion he must have organised this pick up with the lads.

I went to have a look and saw a completely naked woman sprawled against the wall. One of the officers had an open hose reel and was hosing her down with cold water. There was a huge volume of water everywhere. Everybody cheered and yelled. This was a disaster for me! I was employed by the (Home Office) and not by any Fire Brigade. The Duty Officer (whose room was on the ground floor) was now on his way up the stairs as there was a tremendous amount of noise generated by all the Officers. It was way past midnight.

Two doors on either side of the corridor were barred by broom handles. I knew that the duty officer would bang and try to enter the corridor, which he duly did. For me, this was scary. I didn't say anything, and I was thinking about how to escape from this. I waited a few seconds or maybe a minute and this time I knew he would go to the other side and enter that way (which he must have done). Cautiously, I opened the double doors and made my way down the soggy, dripping carpet, ran to my Nissen hut and went to bed.

In the morning, it felt as if someone had died. All officers walked apart from each other. I thought this was strange, but I knew there had to be consequences for what happened last night. After breakfast, I collected my vehicle and did my daily duties. After an hour or so, my boss called me into his office (this was quite a distance from my workplace). As I drove to his office, I knew what was coming.

I was in a dilemma. To lie or tell the truth, or just answer a yes or no to his questions. I walked into his office and sat down.

He was engrossed in writing. Eventually he looked up at me and asked if I took a vehicle to Cheltenham and I said "yes." This has to be OKed by a senior Officer which it was not, but that was not the issue. He asked if I knew anything about last night. I said "yes."

"What?" he asked in a stern voice.

"I took them to their billets at approximately12:00 but you can check with the logbook which is in the vehicle."

He then asked me "Did you know about a woman in the back of the vehicle?"

"No!"

"Okay you can go."

I went on to do my work only to see all the students I worked with in a very sombre mood as they were interrogated. I think this took all day. The next day they talked to me and wanted me to tell them what I said to the boss, which I did, and you could see the relief on their faces. There was a lot of water damage to all the bedsit rooms in this complex (and the cost would be horrendous). This happened two thirds through the course of 11 months, which I think was relevant as to why nobody was sent home.

Consequences were surely on their records!

RESCUE – TRAPPED IN CAR

Magnesium

The fire college was purposely built for the training of fire service personnel on an old RAF airfield to give special experience in dealing with exceptional circumstances, such as ship fires, oil tanker and road tankers on fire, plus purposely built buildings from 1 to 4 stories high. All buildings had reinforced windows, which could withstand high temperatures, as they were water cooled, while the fires were raging inside.

What happened next was not an exercise.

One Friday at 11:55, I was heading for my lunch when I noticed smoke from one of the above-mentioned buildings. I headed full speed towards the smoking building as I knew there was no exercise being run; classes had been wound down for the weekend. There were a number of ground crew hanging around and 2 or so lads were running out hoses. As I approached the smoking building, I wound down my window and shouted out:

"Magnesium do not to put water on!"

Magnesium is a very violently explosive material when alight. Plus gives out large amount of ultraviolet light when on fire especially when volumes of water used. i.e. Analogue cameras use flashbulbs using magnesium to take pictures in the dark.

But "He who must be obeyed" (The Commandant) was giving orders to the ground crew. I noted his car was not many feet away from this building as I swung my vehicle down the runway at maximum speed to the living quarters where the senior officer having his lunch. He was directly in charge of me and running of the teaching programme. On arrival, I banged on the door hard. The door eventually opened, and I yelled at him: "This is an emergency. Get in the vehicle!"

We then headed as fast as we could towards the building. As we approached the building, (we were approximately 50 plus yards away) we were greeted with a spectacular once-in-a-lifetime experience. (I usually have my camera with me, but not this time, of course. Sod's law).

There were 5, 15 to 24 foot long by 8-to-10-inch jets of brilliant blinding white light, accompanied by an almighty explosion. At this point, we were coming around where the Commandant's car was. At that moment, a huge manhole cover was coming through the window of the 2nd floor and landed inches away from the Commandant's car. This idiot got into his car and drove off.

The ground floor of this building was used for the storage of a very large volume of magnesium, (machined splintering). The Commandant, being the top man, should have known better not to medal that does not concern him. It's a difficult material to set alight and the building was locked, as far as I knew, Another story not from me. This all happened a few weeks before I left the college. That's all I know.

FOAM DEMONSTRATION

MY LIFE ON THE LINE

At The Fire College, the fire ground crew were instructed to prepare an oil tanker full of water ("oil") that has turned on its side on a bendy road. On the side of the road was a slight incline of approx. 15 to 20 degrees, which had small trees. This exercise was carried out numerous times in the year.

On this occasion, I was with the main instructor. I requested to attend, which was granted under one condition: not to leave the instructor's side, at a reasonable distance behind everyone as he wanted to observe this particular exercise. I adhered to that.

I was recently given duties to look after this contraption called "Tirfor." It was an intriguing tool. I vaguely recall there were 3 types, (could have been more) of different pulling powers.

This particular day taught me a practical lesson as to why there is a discipline structure in the Fire service. Every fire man, woman, officer, has a duty to maintain safety at all times.

As the exercise was progressing to recover the tanker, an extremely loud command was given "STILL" followed by "DOWN". The next instance I was on my back (the Officer pulled my legs from under me). I heard a whistling sound above my head and a young tree nearby of approximately 4- 6 inches in diameter was cut down by a snapped steel cable, from this apparatus called Tirfor.

There were no injuries, thank goodness. After all the commotion settled down, which took a day or two as everyone had to write down what they saw and did. The Senior Fire Officer (who was in charge of me) wanted the service record of the offending cable as this was the focal point of the investigation, which I promptly gave. Some days or weeks passed before I heard the result of the formal investigation. The outcome of this found the steel cable to be faulty by the manufacturer and in no way was I to blame.

ROAD ACCIDENT EXERCISE

ME FAR RIGHT WITH STATION OFFICERS

Midweek Entertainment

I was now fully involved with the instructors' daily duties, running of the three courses by making all equipment and needs available to the students while at the college. I found myself somewhat deceived one evening by two London Station Officers who were on a 4-week course.

One lunch time, two officers approached me with a request to use the movie projector in the main teaching block. I thought nothing of it, so I agreed. He thanked me and both continued with their lunch. After lunch, I continued with my duties. While I was in my makeshift office-come-storeroom, one of the officers approached me. He asked if I could have it set up the next day at 20.00 hours. This request was highly unusual, and out of teaching hours.

"Yes," I said, but I was somewhat dubious now. I said I would ask The Boss.

I talked to the Senior Officer. He wanted to know a few details, such as what course he was on etc. He looked at some paperwork and said OK.

This particular day was Movie Day and starts at 19.30 hours. Usually, a blockbuster film and free for all. I went to most of them, but not this time as I thought nothing of it helping students.

I was in the teaching hall setting up (around 19.40ish) the 16 mm Projector. As anticipated, this officer, plus 3 or maybe 4 others, turned up and promptly arranged the large room. It felt strange; I asked this officer what the hell was going on? I was not privy to anything apart from setting up the projector. He handed me a large tin reel.

"Hell! What is this?" I said in a loud voice. Before I could bring a halt to the proceedings, I realised there must have been 50-plus students all eager, shouting, and rushing to come in. I noticed the other officer was taking money.

The Station Officer who organised this had told me: "Not to worry! We will see you, okay?" He was keen to get going. The room was full of smoke, swearing, shouting, laughing. I could hardly move to operate the projector. This film turned out to be a one-hour coloured porn film. There was a huge amount of noise.

I shouted, " Keep quiet!" to no avail. I was deceived BIG TIME and there was no escaping for me. Halfway through the film, the Duty Officer Pushed his way in and switched the lights on. Total silence! I froze! I cannot recall what happened next few minutes. The Duty Officer was no other than a Teaching Officer from the Road Accident Course. He saw me, and at that moment, he did not know how to react. He must have been persuaded to stay and watch the remainder of the film.

The problem came to light the next day, as no one apart from a handful of students watched the blockbuster film. I vaguely recall some gossip was going round regarding another event that had taken place that was not authorised.

The film was illegally extracted from Soho in London, by Fire Officers who had been inspecting premises at the time. It was my luck that the Duty Officer was known to me. He knew quite well the consequences if it was known that he was involved. He did approach me with an angry face. I made it quite clear that I was deceived, also I had prior permission to use the equipment, and that calmed him down somewhat.

I cannot recall what happened to the film or how much money passed hands.

Part 2:

Travel

I took this job as I was somewhat disillusioned at the Fire college. I constantly had to drive here, there, and everywhere, doing in excess of 30 miles a day in a confined area as everything was spread out.

This job was driving a bus with 30 plus passengers across Europe and onto India. This took 3 months of sightseeing across many countries, then 14 to15 days back to London.

England To India

Kevin and I were the drivers of a 40-seater coach taking a 3-month sightseeing trip, travelling from London to Delhi in the late 60s. There was a mixture of male and female individuals, age ranging 19 to 65. Most of them were travelling to Australia, some to the far east and elsewhere. The nationalities numbering up to10.

This story starts as we were exiting the Turkish border to Syria at approximately 15:00 hours. I promptly got all passports and paperwork to the authorities, as requested, before the office closed for the day. After about an hour or so, we (drivers) were a short distance from the Passport Office, when we were confronted by 3 military personnel shouting at us and pointing at the passports. They wanted to see this American individual.

We scouted around looking for this individual and a few minutes later we found him. We told him that the military wanted to see him. Can you imagine what happened next?

They got hold of hi; they did not say a word, just frogmarched him to the barbed wire gate, opened it and literally threw him into "No man's land" and they promptly locked the gate. He was shortly followed by his suitcase, which flew over the gate. Now this young man was complaining bitterly, and whining for what must have been an hour or so.

Kevin and I walked to the gate where he was. Kevin told him: "Go back to Istanbul and have that Israeli stamp removed, as we told you to. You kept on bleating that nobody would touch your passport. We will see you in Tehran".

He shouted at us; "What am I going to do tonight? I can't sleep out here!"

"You have no option but to do just that," Kevin replied.

A number of passengers complained to us that we were too hard on him. Kevin abruptly told them to "shut up" as we had no control in this compound. The military of the land has complete control over everything and everybody in this compound, and that is the end of it.

The next day, (I believe it was around noon), we got out of this compound and headed out into Syria. We got to a place called Hims in the early evening and settled down in a local hotel.

The hotelier was very hospitable; he invited us for tea and evening meal in the restaurant. The drivers always got free food and drinks as they brought a large volume of customers. I had no idea what kind of food he would dish out for us.

We had a local drink; I can't remember exactly what it was, but it was defiantly not alcohol. Some minutes later, a large bowl full of sheep's eyes, mounted pyramid style, were placed in front of us, no more than 3 feet away. Just imagine! Eyes staring at me from whatever angle you are looking at. I was screaming inside thinking, "No, no I am not going to eat this!"

I excused myself, as I wanted to go to the bathroom. What bathroom? A Hole in the ground.

That did not stop me from getting out of this restaurant. I left Kevin and the passengers to enjoy himself with the eyes, if that was their idea of enjoyment, and I went to hit the sack.

The next day we headed for Damascus, only to find that we took a wrong turn and went down a minor road, past a small Guard Hut where two guards were looking at us rather perplexed. It was strange, going down this tiny-weenie road, but then, some minutes later, we saw a sign saying: Tripoli 120 km.

"What? Tripoli is in Lebanon!"

"Oh Hell!"

We stopped, turned around and put our foot down without stopping for these two guards, who had no idea what to do seeing a bus headed back into Syria. Everybody was relieved that we came out with no problems. We eventually arrived in Damascus, where everybody seemed to enjoy themselves. I believe we stayed for two days, but I cannot be certain.

The next day, of all days, was the most dangerous and frightening. No! not frightening, but anxious for the passengers at the unknown; the uncertainty of the outcome of this day.

The day started normally with another coach in tow, which literally had no more than five people on board. The driver was a good friend of Kevin, that is why he was tagged along with us.

A little bit about the topography—everywhere you looked, there was sand. It was very hazy and hot. We were driving in a desert on hard sandy ground to the passport control office. In reality, the border is some 6 or so hour's drive in the middle of nowhere, with heat in excess of 40 degrees and white glaring sand on both sides of a black tarmac road. It magically turned into a black straight line as it disappeared into the haze.

We left Damascus behind on a well-paved tarmac road for Iraq. Eventually we got to the point where we had to turn off and drive a few kilometres to where the passport control office was.

All went smoothly with documentation at Passport Control. Everybody was counted on board and ready to rock and roll.

Eventually, I noticed that the track we took to get here was heading totally in the wrong direction, so I suggested: "Let's follow this track along the pylons as they seem to head towards the main road."

A short while later, it became apparent that these pylons were not connected to the road. We needed to get back on the road; and we were looking for a way to do this.

We got over this brow of a small hill.

"OH SHIT!" (An awful lot of swear words were uttered by nearly everybody). We all knew that we were in big trouble. We had hit upon an air force compound!

As we approach this military compound, we were immediately surrounded by military personnel in jeeps numbering 12 or so, fully armed. We (the two buses) were escorted to the compound.

All of us were ordered off the buses. An order was given to put all cameras on some plastic sheeting. I did not move from my bus. Kevin was driving, and he was marched off with the other driver into the compound and we did not see them for what seemed like a few hours.

Kevin and I had made an arrangement back in London that if either of us left the briefcase behind, the other one would look after it. This was paramount as all documents and money for the trip were in this case. So, I got hold of it and sat on the internal bonnet of the bus, the briefcase on my knees.

I can only recall that a soldier (of what rank I had no idea) ordered me in pigeon English to "get off the coach and leave the briefcase". He repeated this several times. This I did not do. He got his rifle off his shoulder and pointed it at my chest and repeated the words.

All the passengers who were outside in the midday sun (40+ deg.) were screaming at me to do just what the soldier ordered me to do. I shouted at the passengers to mind their own business; I was dealing with this in my own way. I looked into the soldier's eyes and shouted "shoot! shoot! you bastard".

He just lowered the rifle and slung it over his should, then started to rummage around on the bus looking everywhere, for what I have no idea at this time.

Now, I happened to look at the other bus and there was an officer doing the same thing. A few minutes passed, maybe half an hour, before this officer entered my bus and ordered me in his pigeon English to "Get off the bus and leave the briefcase".

I did not comply, so he drew his pistol out of his holster and held it against my temple and uttered the same command. Everybody outside was shouting at me to "let go of briefcase and come out of the bus."

I shouted at this officer, "Shoot me! Go on, shoot me!"

He did not, for obvious reasons.

The army gathered up all the cameras and took them away. Sometime later, the cameras were returned minus the films. I was very annoyed (putting it mildly) about that because I had a lot of photographs which were taken from places I had previously missed.

I cannot recollect how long we actually stayed at this military compound. Kevin returned with the other driver, and we were told to get out of this compound and headed onto the highway, which was 30 kilometres away. When we did get to the Iraqi border, we drove into the compound and proceeded to Iraqi passport control.

Only then did we find out why the army officer wanted me off the bus and leave the briefcase. The other driver had all of his documents and money stolen, which was disastrous for him. He could not move out of this country without paperwork. We, the drivers, made a decision that Kevin and his friend make a U-turn for the air force compound and try to solve the dilemma they were in; that they did.

LUNCH BREAK IN EUROPE

PASSENGERS HELP TO MAKE BYPASS

LARGER IMAGE OF TASK AHEAD IN EAST OF
TURKEY. PASSENGERS VERY OBLIGING

Hospital

1971

My passport had only 2 empty pages left. I had to resolve this before I could leave India. I needed a new passport; that was clear. This should have been a straightforward task, instead a bureaucratic nightmare was awaiting me.

Let me explain. The British Embassy in New Delhi, India, was a huge complex at that time, the biggest, with a hospital. It was surrounded by a high wall. Along the outside wall, there stretched a human chain of half a mile (maybe more) of people all trying to enter the visa and passport department, which were in the same large room. All were prepared to camp overnight, as this department only works 2 to 3 hours a day and not every day. When I got to the front gate with my hired Tuktuk (a 3-wheeler), I proceeded to the front of the queue as none wanted the passport section and promptly applied for a new passport.

A live entertaining show for the locals was to be had, and they loved it. They all tried to crowd into this room to see the entertainment. A lot of laughter and shouting and smiles as the bantering between me and this bureaucratic pompous of a Clarke. He had taken already the money and given me a receipt and only asked for my birth certificate at the last moment before issuing it, (I saw a glimpse of a passport in his hand).

I tried in vain to explain that this was not practical, as my birth certificate was at home and no sane man would travel with it. He insisted that I could not have the passport issued to me without a birth certificate. At this point Kevin (a New Zealander) arrived and wanted to know what the holdup was. I explained. Kevin turned round to the Clarke and said, "I am a

New Zealander and got a 6-month British Passport as mine run out in Iran". The Clarke told Kevin to be quiet, this had nothing to do with him.

I said, "This is not logical. I have here in my hand a passport that is a legal document telling you that this is ME and you agreed. Yet! You will not budge."

Now, quite clearly there was an impasse.

Thinking as to why this was, I have come to the conclusion that they were simply being discriminatory due to my non-English accent.

For half an hour (maybe more) we argued, then eventually he succumbed.

At long last, I had my passport: valid for three months only. Yes, I was peeved and very angry! This saga was planted deep in my brain and never left me to this day. I got my own back in due course on this stupid bureaucratic bungling individual (at what cost, I will explain later).

We departed Delhi with a full bus. I believe it was mid to late afternoon, and we were heading up to the northern border of India and Pakistan. Kevin was driving and a few hours into the drive, I told him that I would have some shut eye on the inflatable bed which was at the back of the bus on the floor for a few hours, so far as I know as I was in the land of nod.

The next thing I knew, I was catapulted on my bed and awoke wrapped around the gearstick next to Kevin's legs. I kept my eyes shut and waited for the movement to stop before I opened or moved from lying down position. At that precise moment, a piece of something hit my left eye. I had no idea that it was glass which caused the injury.

All lights were out and total darkness. After a hell of a lot of commotion, I told Kevin that I would try to bring the lights on. I had a reasonable amount of confidence and knowledge that this could be done as I had checked all fuses and rewired some of it prior to departing London.

After a few minutes I got the centre lights of the coach working and that made a huge difference to the morale of the passengers, plus it gave the nurse whom we had on board more of a chance to diagnose any injuries, which were very few. We had one girl with a cut above the bridge of her nose and another with a nasty cut on her knee.

Time for me was not the issue, to be frank. I really cannot recall much more of what was going on as my head was aching and I had no idea that I was badly injured in my left eye. Things were becoming a little hazy and my memory is not too clear about how long I stayed on the bus. It became apparent that I had to get medical treatment for this. Kevin managed to get a vehicle or a taxi or whatever and bundled me and this girl into the taxi.

The cause of this accident was due to a lorry being parked around a bend on trestles without lights and no prior warning of any kind given. Kevin told me later on how sorry he was for causing such misery and pain. This was not necessary as it was not his fault. One cannot see around bends in the middle of the night and in the rainy conditions. So far as I am concerned, I have and never will blame him for what happened to my eye.

I told him to give me my passport. I refused to take money. By the way, I was totally blindfolded and had a headache of all headaches. And I had every intention of getting my own back on this bureaucratic of a Clarke at the British Embassy in Delhi.

Sometime later, not knowing time or distance, I arrived at the British Embassy blindfolded and angry. My head was giving me a lot of trouble. I eventually got into the embassy after being directed to see this official.

He told me: "The embassy had a hospital, but it was only for the staff."

"What?" I shouted. This made me even angrier. I demanded to see the GP or doctor at the embassy. This in due course was reluctantly granted, and a doctor arrived and talked to me. He told me he was just a general practitioner and nothing else, but he knew an ophthalmologist and would give me the directions to get there. I immediately replied that I was unable to see where I'm going, let alone find my way across the city with my eyes covered. He agreed that he would do what he could.

This embassy official came and took me to the taxi and gave the driver instructions to take me to the ophthalmologist, which he did. On arrival, he helped me up some stairs into the surgery, whereupon the nurse told me to remove the bandage.

I promptly asked whether there were lights on and the window open. The reply was "yes".

I said: "The bandage stays on until lights go off and the curtains drawn. My bandage has been on me for the last 12 to 24 hours or so."

With this commotion going on (I think) ophthalmologist entered and complied with my wishes. He took the bandage off and, lo-and-behold, he might as well have stabbed me with a knife into my eye. The pain was excruciating. With just a glance, he determined the seriousness of my left eye. As he re bandaged my head, he shouted for the taxi driver and instructed to take me immediately to the hospital. He promptly did and left me at the entrance, I think with a piece of paper in hand.

By now, I was at my wits' end. I could not think, nor could I speak coherently. All I wanted was to lie down and get this headache of all headaches out of me, but that was not to be. I was physically blocked by a policeman who wanted to know all about the incident. I must have given him some shit remarks as I lifted the bandaged from my watering right eye and peeked to find somewhere to lie down. I saw a stretcher leaning against the wall. Oh! I remember a welcoming feeling coming over me as I ventured onto this stretcher and lay down. I was in ecstasy.

Some time passed; I could not tell you how long. I heard a familiar voice asking about me; it was Kevin. He had backtracked and found me. That was a welcome sound! I shouted: "Over here".

He wanted to know if anybody had seen me. I said: "No, I can't get past the bloody policeman!" Next moment I heard a huge commotion and Kevin slamming the policeman against the wall and shouting abuse at him. I could not take much more noise and general commotion. Finally, I received some medical attention as one doctor after another came to me and wanted to help.

With my limited first aid experience back in England, I wanted nothing but an ophthalmologist, which I duly got as the next individual happened to be the Top Ophthalmologist. He was the man.

I said: "Do what you have to do."

The nurse injected me in the eye then and there. It felt like a nail being pushed into the eye (that's how blunt it felt) and

41

around the eye, another injection into the arm. Now I was in the land of nod.

I came round in an annex to the main operating theatre. I looked around and found them operating on eyes; I saw a head that had a huge pair of spectacles where his eyes should have been — instead; they were cradled in them with the cord entering the brain. I was fascinated, but I was soon put down by another injection and that was that.

The next thing I can recall was talking either in my sleep or I was awake but was not aware that both eyes were covered. I was talking to Kevin, and it seemed to me that he wanted my passport so he could transfer the coach to his passport.

I recall that this conversation about all sorts of nonsense was very vivid but very strange as there was nothing I could focus on mentally or physically. When one wakes up in the morning and opens one's eyes, one instinctively knows that they are awake. You have an immediate reference. After coming round from being anaesthetised, with one's eyes bandaged up, you have no idea if you are asleep or awake. That is extremely bewildering. I cannot recall exactly when my bandages were removed, but my right eye was uncovered more or less immediately or the next day or so. I do recall a lot of tears was coming out of the right eye.

Soon after the operation, the British Embassy official came by to see if everything was okay and I said no. I needed money for food, which was the truth, as I told Kevin not to give me any money. The Embassy official was not willing to part with money as this was not Home Office policy, but in this case he did give me a small amount of money and he made it quite clear he wanted this money back. I agreed, (but I never did). I ordered food which did not have any curry in. Well, put it this way, it is not possible to have food in India that does not taste of curry.

The hospital supplied yellowish slop. There is a combination of rice and curry, or curry and rice, and the colour is a disgusting greenish yellow slop. No way on this earth will I eat that crap.

The following day, a girl of 9 to 12 was placed in a bed next to me and this was a huge jolt to reality for me. The surgeon and his students examined her. Her father was by her side all day and all night until I left. I overheard the conversation with the father pleading with the surgeon, saying he would give anything to save his daughter's sight. The surgeon told him that it was imperative for the eye to be removed, due to infection setting in and entering the brain.

The father told him: "that would make her totally blind!"

The surgeon said: "That is so, but it is better than being dead because she would be dead within six months if not sooner if the eye was not removed."

Here was I, taking life rather frivolously, when such a tragic and painful situation was no more than 3 feet from me. This situation is still very vivid in my brain, and it brings tears recalling such a sad time.

One night, (I can't recall the exact time nor date) I believe that I was on the third floor of this huge wing of the hospital. This wing consisted of four wards on either side of this long corridor (no doors to the wards) and 8 beds to a ward. I was placed in the 2nd ward at the far-right hand next to the window. I could see, during daylight, monkeys on the tree at times. Diagonally across the corridor was a room where the nurses hung out. Next to that was a smaller room, holding all the auxiliary items that nurses need. Amongst that was a heater (it turned out to be a gas boiler).

On this night in question, there was a huge explosion and a cloud of dust billowed towards me. I sat up. Nobody got alarmed apart from nurses, who were scuttling around checking on patients. I waited for the dust cloud to settle, then got out of bed and headed to the centre of the corridor. I noticed with very little light around me a huge crack in the ceiling something like 1.5 to 2 inches the full length of the hospital wing and the wall facing outside next to where the nurses were was blown out completely.

I promptly got my belongings (which were few) and proceeded to go downstairs. 2 Nurses rushed after me calling out "Where are you going?"

My reply was simple: "To sleep on a stretcher on the floor at the entrance to the hospital!", which I did. Nurses and minders kept interfering with my trying to sleep, telling me to go back to bed as everything was all OK. I told them to go away (politely); I was going to sleep here. The next day, structural engineers came in and examined the structure top and bottom and deemed it to be safe.

Several days passed. Knowing that my stay was coming to an end at the hospital in Delhi, I said my goodbyes to the surgeon (who gave me a letter to pass on to the doctors in the UK) and to the nurses, then headed off to the British Airways office to get my ticket. I then got onto the bus for the airport.

When the bus arrived at the airport, I cannot remember how long I waited before departure, but as soon as I got to the departure area, I had to go through a police check.

What transpired next is very clearly embedded in my head yet again. This policeman (thick as two planks) took hold of my passport and noticed no entry stamp on this new passport. He promptly wanted my old passport, which I gave him. Now! he was in a quandary. He wanted to know where the bus was. I said it was out of the country, but he could not understand this at all. The bus's entry to India was clearly stamped on my old passport. On the back page, it stated that the bus has been transferred to Kevin. Obviously, this policeman was not on the bright side, and it just did not click in his brain that the bus was not with me. I got a little annoyed with him and shouted at him not to be so bloody stupid, but to no avail. He demanded to know where the bus was. Now, there was a native Indian man, way past my height and he was carrying a cello the size of me. He was annoyed at the policeman for taking such a long time. I asked this chap to explain to him in their native tongue what the situation was. He promptly did, and that seemed to do the trick.

I must give credit to British Airways for their service. When I got onto the plane, I was pampered. They made a bed for me and told me I could lie down, which I did. They supplied me with aspirin, which I took, and I promptly fell asleep.

I was woken up by a command the loudspeaker bellowed out, I shouted " bloody hell!"
The stewardess came around and asked: "What's the problem?"
I said, "Can this loudspeaker (directly over my head) be disconnected please?"
 She said she would ask the flight engineer. We took off and shortly after the flight engineer came along and disconnected the loudspeaker. I settled down for a nice sleep for a couple of hours or so. I was given a meal and a nice hot drink; the captain came to see me and asked if anything can be done, and I said no. He told me to ask the steward if I needed anything. Approximately 2 hour or so before getting into Heathrow, someone asked me if anybody was meeting me and I replied as far as I was aware, no. They asked me if they could phone home. "Yes, please!"
Which they did.

On arrival at Heathrow, they asked me if I could walk down the steps and I said yes, but as soon as I got to the steps, the whole world was spinning and it was obvious to them that I was not safe to go down the steps by myself. I stayed in the aircraft for a while; and they arranged for a wheelchair, which duly arrived, and I was coaxed down the steps onto the wheelchair, armed with my passport and a little luggage of dirty laundry. I was more or less wheeled straight through to the car without stopping to where my brother was waiting. British Airways did follow up by phoning mum and dad to see if I arrived safely, which was very nice of them.

My Father took the letter from the hospital in Delhi to my GP and he promptly told me to go straight to hospital, which I did. I was given a bed close to the entrance to the ward and told to undress and get straight into bed and stay there. Now this was a very miserable time for me. The curtains were drawn so no day light could get in and only one 60-watt light bulb in the whole ward was on and that's it. All I had were my memories.

The next day I decided to have a bath as I hadn't had to wash for a few days, and I must have stank. I picked a time and filled the bath which directly opposite the ward and promptly had to wash it was heaven.

The next thing I heard was "a commotion wanted to know where I was?" Someone banged on the door and shouted: "Will you please get out of the bath immediately and into bed!"

"Okay, in a while," I said.

"NO! NOW THIS INSTANT!"

I got into bed and was told off by a nurse or matron or whoever. The next day, the surgeon came around and told me off.

"You should ask the nurse to wash you".

I replied, "Nonsense, I was quite capable of washing myself, and anyway, what's all the fuss about?"

He replied: "Having a hot bath was bad for your eye as the blood pressure would damage the eye".

"If you told me that in the first place, then I would have complied!"

He agreed and that was that.

For one solid week, I was told to lie still. The eye was not stable, and he had to remove the stitches. This was an extremely delicate operation. It needed a stable eye and to reach to that point I would have to cooperate with them. This was extremely hard, but after all, I had zero option.

I was told by the surgeon that there was a problem and as far as he was concerned, there was no way he or anybody could know what the outcome was and only time would tell. He told me that there was a foreign body in my eye, and that gave him great concern.

After several attempts, all 14 stitches were removed. I was eventually discharged but kept under close supervision for several months. Some time passed and I had to go to Birmingham eye hospital as they wanted to see what could be done. They told me the next year or so would be a deciding factor if a rejection was going to happen. The more time passed, the less chance of rejection, which in hindsight was good news.

Syrian/Iraqi Border Compound

I am fairly confident that my memory serves me well. It was late afternoon, and we were too late for passport processing, so we had to stay in the locked compound overnight. The border and passport control compound were in the desert miles from the nearest town or village. Early next morning, I headed to passport control armed with all the paperwork and a briefcase; I was in a large hall, filled with a huge number of people, some drivers, but more officials and border guards, police and no doubt lookout spies. I waited my turn in a short queue.

Eventually, I was beckoned forward by a middle-aged man, who was taken aback by the volume of paperwork I had placed in front of him. I sat down and watched for several minutes as he processed my passport. This was painfully slow. I had to speed things up! I reached into the briefcase on my lap and took out a paper bag out (in which was a copy of Mayfair magazine). I pulled the sheets of paper out of the bag, giving all passengers information needed for the official to log it down later, as all he had to do was to stamp all passports.

I then slipped the paper bag under the table, hitting his leg on purpose at the same time giving him the typed sheets of paper. He looked at me with a stern face and seemed annoyed that I was still tapping his leg. He looked down, then immediately grabbed the paper bag open it. His face lit up and gave me a broad smile at the same time tried to grab my knee. I pulled myself back quickly. Here was a happy man! In no time, he was stamping all passports. It's amazing what an adult magazine can achieve in an Arab Country.

At long last, we were on the road to Baghdad. We soon found out how annoying the military is and how the country is controlled, as we were constantly stopped by them. They asked everyone what their occupation was in broken English. This was ridiculous. Everyone made up all sorts of nonsense, such as brain surgeons, astronauts, etc. It was clearly a futile exercise, as these personnel could not understand what they were being told.

Eventually arriving in Baghdad, all the passengers were extremely thirsty and hungry. It was noon, and the temperature was in the 40s plus. I stopped near a bank and all passengers ran to the shade of the bank to exchange money. Everyone filled in the appropriate paperwork and handed over money with their passport to the clerk, whereupon he placed them in a pile on a shelf behind him in full view of us, and that was that. He just sat at his desk and had some tea of some kind. This was extremely frustrating and difficult to hold one's temper. Several passengers were shouting at him, to no avail.

This country had a compulsory waiting time of at least one hour before any action could be taken by the clerk. Eventually we did get money, whereupon we headed straight for a teahouse of some sort and had some refreshments. The following day (no one wanted to stay in this country) we headed out of the city where we immediately got pestered again by the oppressive military regime every 20 to 30 minutes. We headed north to the Iranian border and on arrival everyone gave a loud cheer and clapped our hands.

A few hours passed as we were going through passport control. Yes! I used the brown paper bag again, entering Iranian passport control, then headed into Iran.

It was the start of a major headache for me driving down this mountain range. I was coming down at ever-increasing speed and noticed the brakes were not performing as they should; I changed rapidly down into 2nd gear and at this point the brakes became useless. The challenge was driving the bus without a conventional braking system working. This was serious for me.

The Exhaust Brake was the only tool available to me, but increasingly difficult to operate as I needed my 2 hands on steering wheel, lucky there was a passenger who jumped up and asked if he could help.

I said in a loud voice: " YES PLEASE!"

That he did. When told, he pulled the leaver to operate exhaust brake.

(For those who do not know what "Exhaust Brake" is or does, it literally shuts off gasses escaping from the engine, causing the engine to slow down the vehicle).

We eventually stopped by using the exhaust brake upon reaching a reasonably level and straight part of the road. On examining the whole rear double wheel assembly, I found it to be dangerously hot and smelt of burning rubber. I was concerned that I would be stuck without four wheels (or shall I say, tyres!). Quick action had to be taken! Looking to my right: mountain. To my left there was a reasonable step valley of 50 to 100 meters. Fortunately, there was a brook down this bank where we managed to get some water to cool the tyres and the wheels. Sometime later, I examined the inside lining of the brake shoes and found them completely useless as the heat had damaged the brake linings to a point where a screwdriver could penetrate the lining right down to the metal.

Some hours later, after cooling the wheels, I continued to Isfahan without any mishap. We arrived midafternoon and stayed here for two nights. Early the following day, we headed to Tehran. It took us some eight hours to arrive, and by this time (plus 400 miles on using exhaust brake), I was exhausted from driving and thinking at least 4 to 5 vehicles ahead. I had a few near collisions but managed very well under the circumstances. Driving a bus into the city with failing brakes and having to negotiate traffic, as well as finding the way to the hotel where Kevin would be, was exhausting. On arriving outside the hotel, I stumbled into the lobby, where I found Kevin drinking a beer.

I said to him: "I need sleep now. Be careful! Caution—extreme caution—no brakes on bus! Faulty brakes!" Then I fell asleep on a very old soft three setter settee. I did not wake up until the following morning.

Kevin was at the garage, which happened to be a major Ford agent. The main technician nearly went through the brick wall (or so I was told) by not believing that the brakes were faulty. Only then did he remove the brake fluid and the assisted vacuum pump and replace all the brake shoes. That solved that.

Border Post Afghanistan

While Kevin was doing all the paperwork with border officials, I went walkabout around the perimeter, only to find absolutely desolations. I ambled around the ramshackle mud construction huts and then back to the main border office. As I approached the office, I heard a loud sound.

"Pssst! psst!"

Looking around, I saw no one. Then I spotted a grubby hand beckoning to me from the corner of the building. Being curious, I approached the individual. I was greeted by one of the officials wanting to sell me some hashish, a nice big, black block. 4 by 8 inch for $5. I refused straightaway, but word had got round already as passengers bought packets of this and promptly got smashed out of their heads on it.

The same day, at midafternoon, we stopped at a hotel in the middle of nowhere to rest up for the night drive of 13 plus hours to Kabul. We arrived at a first-class hotel (so it seemed), with300 odd bedrooms. It was totally kitted out with a kitchen, reception etc and yet lacking power of any kind. A caretaker sat cross-legged on the floor. He had a small wood fire lit with a kettle on in the reception! Lunacy. Who do you think built this? The Russians.

We took over this hotel for the 4 to 5 hours. Everyone bar one or two were there, congregated around the large swimming pool. Yes, it had water, but stagnant water. There was algae floating here and there. I recall two took a dip, but the rest dangled their legs into the water. I was thinking: who filled this, and where did they get this volume of water from? Very strange!

At 17:00 hours, it was time to start the drive to Kabul. All were accounted for and onboard, we headed back onto the main road. I was driving for about an hour or so when Kevin told me to keep a sharp lookout for a log the full width of the road.

I asked him: "What kind of sign or warning would I be looking out for?"

He said: "No warning, there is nothing."

It was approximately 22:00 hours, and I was driving for quite a few hours at a steady speed of 50 mph when suddenly, within a blink of an eye, I saw this log and hit it. Everybody in the bus and everything that was not fixed to the bus went everywhere. I stopped on the other side of the log. Kevin came up to me and said: "let's see the damage."

I got out with him and mind you; it was pitch black outside and got underneath with a torch and inspected the underneath. I expected severe problems, but nothing too serious. One or two springs, I think.

We took this time to have a WC stop. Everybody who needed one please go to the back of the Bus. Ladies to the left, Gents to the right, off you go. Approximately 15- 20 minutes later, we all settled down again and proceeded on to Kabul, where we would do repairs and have breakfast. First, we had a refuelling stop at Kandahar. This was around 01:30 hours. This was a long refuelling process as one had to pump by hand in total darkness, apart from a dimly lit oil lantern given to me by the pump attendant that kept me company.

It was an unforgettable experience driving towards Kabul at night. There was no vegetation at all, and in front of me was the wide-open expanse of a starlit sky. As the miles rolled by, the sky turned ever so slightly brighter, illuminating the faint silhouette of the hilly and mountainous topography looking to the east. To mark this unforgettable time in my brain, I was listening to Simon and Garfunkel music on my tape deck. It was perfect. Just perfect.

CHIEF OF FIRE SERVICE IN AFGHANISTAN (Kabul).

Chief of the Fire Service

While I was at fire college Moreton in Marsh. I came across this individual who was on a clerical course from a country called Afghanistan. I got to know him reasonably well during lunch breaks, over his few weeks' stay at the college. He was sitting apart from the rest of the officers, and I made a point to sit with him and talk to him in simple English. He told me that he was the Chief Fire officer of Kabul, and his country needed to modernise the Fire service. We chatted about general topics and things he wanted and needed.

It turned out he wanted the full Fire service manuals of which there were in the region of 10 to12 books. His budget did not allow this. I believe the cost was £100 or thereabout. On one occasion the topic of travel came up. I told him my plans to travel overland to India and see what I can bring for you. He thanked me and we parted. A few weeks, maybe a month or two, I was on my travel through Europe to India.

Arriving in Kabul, and staying a day or two, I walked with this bundle of books to where the fire station was in Kabul. At the locked gate where the fire service was situated was an armed guard who would not let me in. I made a lot of noise and asked, or shall I say, shouted, to no avail.

I could not remember this chaps name, nor would I go away without delivering the books. I made hand gestures with words like "chief' and "salutes". The guard said words and sounds and that sparked my brain with the name of the chief officer.

"Otaki!" I shouted his name as loud as I could. That brought him out of his ramshackle office.

He proceeded towards me, as I was still behind the locked gate. When he recognised me, all hell broke out. Everybody stood to attention. The barbed wire gate was unlocked. He just stood there in total amazement and disbelief for a while, then shaking my hand just could not believe his own eyes, he saw my parcel and picked it up and headed to his office. He could not thank me enough for coming to see him. I said here are the fire service manuals you wanted. He could not open the parcel quick enough, when he saw the complete set. His expression was indescribable.

It was clear to me that this present was not expected to materialise, but it did, and he showed his appreciation by giving me a complete tour of Kabul. I even went to his home and was presented with his hospitality. I was privileged and introduced to his wife and children, which is not usually done in the Muslim family; the wife is kept usually apart from foreigners and visitors. But I was privileged to meet them.

We parted company, and I never saw him or heard of him again, but no doubt that I did do some good to this country if only in a small way.

THE INFAMOUS KHYBER PASS

Delhi Back to London

The 3-month sightseeing trip from England to India was over. Kevin and I had 7-10 days to turn the bus around for the homeward journey. We accomplished this within a week and were on our way with a bus full of fare-paying passengers. This trip home was scheduled to take 14 days. Virtually non-stop apart for refuelling, passport control, plus food stops.

We had numerous nationalities on board, but one Greek individual just did not fit in with the rest of the passengers. He was very uneasy; extremely nervous. I will explain later.

There was an incident which everybody on the bus would remember. This was in the northern part of Turkey, and we suddenly drove onto a non-tarmac road for several miles in heavy rain, when we came across stationary trucks and waited till the rain stopped to investigate why.

We did not have to wait long! Kevin and I got out in thick mud and surveyed the situation. It was bleak! Here there were a variety of trucks all stationary because of one intercontinental truck, heavily laden with goods (we were told 30 plus tons). All axels were buried in mud. This situation immediately transported me back to where I was born in South America. I have seen this before with a 10-ton truck. That took all day to dig it out.

We moved around, talking and surveying the situation for 10-20 minutes. I shortly made a gesture to Kevin to come down to where I was, at a small stream running on bed rock.

I suggested that we get all the passengers involved in moving all these loose stones and rocks and make a makeshift road towards and through the stream.

His comment: "This will not work."

I said: "We only have two options; try to do it or just sit it out, which could take days. I suggest we put it to the passengers and see what happens."

Well, as it turned out, everybody (except one) gave us a hand and made a bypass around this convoy of trucks. A few hours passed doing this.

As soon as it became obvious to the other drivers, (3 of them) one by one they started their trucks getting ready to go to our bypass. I was way ahead of them.

I anticipated this would happen and had a jack handle with me. As soon as I heard the engines start up, I was on the footplate of the leading truck with the handle ready and my head going back and forth. He stopped the engine, knowing full well trouble was at hand.

I stayed on the foot plate until everyone had washed their hands and we were moving slowly down the precarious slope and across the stream; I followed on foot, making sure no truck would try to overtake our bus until we hit hard ground.

We drove into Istanbul right up to our hotel, whereupon we were told that the curfew was in place at six o'clock in the evening. There was a political assassination (or attempted one) of a German diplomat.

The next day was a beautiful sunny day — not a cloud to be seen and sitting in a hotel was lunacy. I told Kevin, "Let's go and have a look at The Blue Mosque".

He said: "They won't let us go".

I said "So what! To hell with them. Let's see what happens."

With my camera in hand, we started off, only to be stopped by the military a few hundred yards from the hotel. They told us (in broken English) to go back to the hotel.

I said "No, I am not going back."

A few minutes later, a senior officer walked up and talked to the junior officer, probably to find out what's going on. The senior officer repeated the command to go back.

My reply was, "How far away was this murder?"

He replied, "Several kilometres away."

I said, "Okay, there's no problem then. We're just going to The Blue Mosque, and it would be perfectly safe."

"No," came the reply.

I said, "if you are worried about our safety, why not let two or three of your soldiers come with us to the Blue Mosque?"

He eventually agreed to do just that. We proceeded to the Blue Mosque with soldiers in tow. Kevin talked to the soldiers while I photographed the odd soldier. They were not impressed and told me to stop.

At that time, I made history. I have photographs of the Blue Mosque with not a soul around and this is on slides (negatives mounted on cardboard frame and it is not digitally altered).

The curfew lasted, thinking back, approximately 24 to 36 hours.

We stayed in Istanbul for 4 days where we did a cleanup of the coach and a full service.

Eventually we headed towards Greece. We got to the border only to find the guards were waiting for us. They were very keen to look for one person.

This quiet individual on the bus was singled out with his case and taken into the office, whereupon the case was opened. I briefly saw precious stones, rings, gold and silver. The border guards told us to leave the office and shut the door and that was that.

At the next stop, Munich in Germany, we dropped off a couple and then headed for Dover.

Before we got onto the ferry, we cleaned inside and outside the coach so as to make it presentable to the UK customs.

We had a passenger from Istanbul, and he happened to be, I think, the owner or part owner of the hotel we used on our trips. I believe he was on route to Canada.

When we got to Dover, an inspection of the bus was carried out by 2 custom officers. I recall one of the customs officers wanted the tool chest down for inspection, so being the driver, I climbed up. I shouted down, " It's bloody heavy! You can have a look if you come up! I unlocked it for you."

The answer came: "No, don't bother, let it be."

I was not aware of what was inside the toolbox except for tools until we got into London and then I had a real fright. Kevin had put a small casket filled full of silver and gold puzzle rings inside the toolbox, or shall I say tool chest, which was on top of the roof rack. Being the driver of the bus takes all responsibilities of the bus and contents.

Words were said in a manor unfit to print.

This could have had grave consequences!

Part 3

Industrial Anecdotes

The stories here are the most memorable and tell of a time after my travels. Most take place in a period of 20 to 30 years, then a short period of employed work at 2 companies. Then unto agency work, followed by 13 years of full employment.

SHORT OF 20 YEARS WITH THE COMPANY!

Take-over

Day 1.

One day all workers were told that the company has been taken over by another company from Birmingham, but production was continuing as normal. A few days later, I was summoned to the director's office. I was expecting something to happen, but not this soon after the takeover. Yes, I was somewhat uneasy and apprehensive. I knocked, opened the door, and walked in. He invited me to draw up a chair, and that I did. The atmosphere was very tense, and he was looking at me sternly. He spoke to me very bluntly and told me that I was being made redundant forthwith. He made a comment that the company would like to make a contract with me. He asked if I would accept.

I replied: "It all depends on what's in the contract?"

He said in so many words: "Can you attend a meeting at 10 o'clock the next day with the works manager? He will negotiate with you the terms of the contract. Will you do this?"

"Yes"! I replied. (Not knowing what I let myself in for). With that, he handed me a brown envelope containing £1000 and public liability insurance in goodwill and wishing me well, and we parted.

Day 2

The following day, in the manager's office, I found this man behind his desk. He was very unpleasant looking, and this put me on guard. I was expecting some kind of timetable and serious negotiations.

Instead, a sheet of paper was placed in front of me to sign. It was more of a dictatorial statement of intent. Negotiating is not the word that sprang to mind. I asked him several questions about this only to be rebuffed and told me in so many words, take it or leave it.

I said, "You are not negotiating, you are dictating, I cannot accept this."

With that, he picked up the phone and talked to the director, slammed the phone down and said, "The Director wants to speak to you".

By now my attitude was very bloody minded. Angry and stone faced, I entered the director's office without knocking. I immediately proceeded to pull up the armchair right in front of him. I could see he was in a foul mood. He immediately told me, in a very strong and forthright voice, that I had undermined the goodwill gesture of £1000 he said he gave me.

"Would you please handover the thousand pounds?" he said.

I kept a straight face and looked him straight into his eyes and said, "What thousand pounds?"

All I have is a public liability insurance certificate, which you can take gladly black. He insisted that I hand back the money straightaway. I repeated "What thousand pounds?"

With that, I got up and moved the armchair back to its original position.

He said, "I'll get my legal department onto you!"

With that, I turned around and left.

As I left the office, I was very pleased with myself for getting £1000 out of this company for nothing. No legal action could be taken or would be taken. That I was sure of, as there was no paper trail, nor signature saying that I received £1000. Yes, I did receive two or three legal letters from a solicitor threatening me with court proceedings, but nothing materialised.

Accident Waiting to Happen

What you are about to read happened while I was not employed by this company. I was told by my good friend.

There were two oil burning furnaces adjacent to each other. Each held approximately one ton of molten metal. My job was to maintain all the equipment, including the two oil-fired furnaces. While I was working on or around the furnaces, during the course of two decades.

I repeatedly told the furnace operators to put their safety equipment on properly. To my knowledge, the company never enforced this safety rule. I did tell them repeatedly.

The Crucibles containing the molten metal were designed to be tilted to 45° allowing the metal to flow out into the mould via elongated channels. At the same time, the casting rig, which held the huge mould, is capable of tilting towards the Crucible full of molten metal. Then the casting rig is put into an upright position and slowly lowered as the metal flows into the mould. The shape of the mould is a big A-frame, one leg of the shape A is 10 feet, while the other one is a shorter 6 foot.

The actual casting was for part of a minesweeper. The part that holds the drive shaft that drives the propeller. The combined weight of mould and casting is in the region of 4-5 tons. On completion of the pouring process, there is now a manual operation.

This means that the operator had to climb on top of the mould, which has molten metal inside the mould. There are numerous (approx. 12 to 15) vents to allow more molten metal to be poured in manually as the casting shrinks.

71

MOULD MADE OUT OF SPECIAL SAND READY TO
CAST

As I have said, I was not there, so don't know how exactly it happened. But I can guess.

One critical part of safety equipment was the boots. The design feature was a quick release mechanism to allow one's foot to be removed from the boot if you needed to do so in an emergency. The difficulty is that the operators were lazy and would not fasten the boots properly, constantly leaving them open.

Being human and working in constant temperature above 50 degrees is intolerable. I do know as I had to refit hydraulic pips etc, many times wild the furnaces were on.

The operator must have held a large ladle of molten metal ready to pour into the casting, that meant his eyes were fixed on the base of the ladle, so he was not paying attention to the boiling vents. I was not told which foot went into which vent of the casting, but I have a very vivid picture of what could have happened.

Now lots of scenarios flying into my brain. Lots of yelling, screams, and running around just horrible. Yes! I was in shock when upon hearing his life changing injury.

OIL FIRED FURNACE

The Shaking Teacup

Memories of My Friend Brian

I was working in my workshop when a supervisor came in and informed me that the overhead (crane motor) had broken down. It had stopped above a lit furnace, in extreme heat. The whole crane could travel across the full length of the Foundry and is constantly in demand. Hence, quick action was required.

The crane control panel was situated between17 to 18 feet above ground level and opposite to where the furnace was lit. This control panel had consisted of two voltages: 440 Volts 3 phase and 12 Volts AC. My co-worker and friend Brian was with me at the time.

His official job title was truck driver, yet he was a capable and multi tasked individual. One asset he had that no other person had that was his physical strength.

He climbed, unaided vertically up the steel shape "H" or "I" beam.

He moved fast to get the ladder. As I got my tools and test equipment and headed inside the factory, the ladder was up and already against the control box for me.

I climbed up the ladder while Brian held the foot of the ladder. In no time, I located and rectified the fault. At that precise moment, I got a nasty electric shock.

I knew that I had to get down the ladder quickly as my body would go into shock. A few moments later, it did.

I shouted out: "Brian, get me hot tea quick!"

He has seen the shock occur and was on his way already.

I sat myself on the floor, which was the safest place, and when Brian handed me the tea, I was shaking reasonably well. I looked up at him, and he was laughing at me. Glancing at my hands, I saw they were shaking violently, and that started me off. I could see the funny side.

A lot of fellow workers were laughing, seeing me sitting on floor and shaking with hot tea flying all over the place. Another tea was given to me as I continued to shake. A few moments later, the shaking subsided.

To continue on the theme of shaking, there was a piece of equipment called a shakeout machine; it is extremely noisy and dusty; it was designed to shake out all the sand and reinforcing wire out of the castings.

Many years later, when Brian, who was a good friend of mine, was ill in the hospital. I went to visit him.

I recall seeing him on the first visit propped up in bed and very subdued.

Seeing him like this brought tears to my eyes. He greeted me and I responded immediately with a silly remark, as I wanted to bring a smile to his face.

"Do you remember the shaking teacup incident?" I said.

A little grin appeared on his face. I said: "You should go onto the shakeout machine and shake this shit illness out!" I said it without thinking, stupid me. But I think I was justified in saying this, as it made him laugh. This, in turn, made me laugh too. At this time, his wife came into see him. I said my farewell and left.

I returned for another visit but was not aware of how seriously ill he was. On entering the hallway and baring right, I saw all his family standing out and inside the room. I thought I was too late and turned around to leave. The family called me back and told me that he was dying. They asked me to go in and see him. I was humbled, and weak at the knees, seeing him. I bent and kissed his forehead and whispered, "farewell my friend". Then I turned around, and shaking my head in disbelief, left the room into the corridor and sobbed against the wall. I think I was out of sight of family. This broke my heart! Writing this switches on my emotions even now, many years later.

I have a very nice picture in my head of my dear friend and work colleague. He used to sing countless 1960 pop songs. "Pretty Woman" by Roy Orbison I believe this was his favourite.

MY FRIEND IN FRONT OF CASTING ON LEFT

BRIAN

Slide Rule verses 1 Penny per Hour

The era is mid 70s and the time of year to have one's appraisal taken. This was done by one of the two Directors. I had just come back from an extended holiday and had been presented with a parting gift. One might say: so, what? Bear with me. Thinking about this puts a smile on my face because of how ridiculous this sounds.

I was called into his office and sat in front of this desk. He was seated at his desk, his head bent over, his nose nearly touching the desk with a magnifying glass up to his eye, looking at the slide rule. I was sitting there twiddling my thumbs and picking up one or two recognisable words as he was talking to himself while calculating my wages.

Eventually, he sat up and told me how things are with the company. He told me that me being away for an extended holiday would hurt the company and this was reflected in the wage increase he was awarding me.

I was half expecting this from him, to deny me taking an extended holiday.

I said "You and your brother, plus the manager, agreed to my extended holiday. You conveniently forgot that I did not take any annual holidays for 2 years."

I pulled my brand-new calculator out of my top pocket and showed this to him. I thanked him for the 1p an hour increase! His expression on seeing a calculator for the first time was magical to me, completely speechless. Just seeing that, I was well pleased with myself!

Local college

One day, the Managing Director called me into his office and instructed me to attend a local college course in electrics. (I was 35 years old), I think in his wisdom (I doubt he had any) he thought I needed more education in this field. Yes! That I did need! But I did not need to be put into the second year of a three-year course for one day a week. Just stupid. I was like a fish out of water.

I had no time to adjust myself for this daunting experience, as I have never attended any such schooling, let alone a college of higher education.

The day came. I was introduced into a class of some 17 to 20 years old. The numbers could have been anywhere between 14 to 20. There was a lot of sniggering calling me names, etc.

I sat most of the days doing nothing! Nothing; just gawping at the blackboard and surroundings. It became apparent to me these lads were apprentices from local companies that meant they had zero knowledge about the physical side of this industry nor how to use tools as the trade union did not allow this to happen, only skilled workers. (how do you get skills?).

The class was in session; I recall the following weeks was nothing more than formula upon formula on the blackboard. I was constantly asked why I was not doing any of them.

"I don't know what the hell you have written!" was my response. That brought the class into a loud laughing session.

No one was doing my job in the foundry, and jobs were piling up. I had to work hard the rest of the week trying to catch up. I never did manage this. This was going on for several weeks.

One day we were told that we would start 6 weeks of practical. That was music to my ears. This day came, and the tables were turned. Everyone in the class, including teacher, was totally dumbfounded as I sprang into action.

The class had to fit a working motor and all electrical accessories and do a wire diagram. This should take you 6 weeks.

I muttered, "Will it hell!"

I did this easily in an afternoon. The college was in a mess regarding equipment and tools. All of the items that students had to use were more or less in a pile underneath the work benches. I was told that my drawing was not up to standard. Thinking back, I said something like: "But nevertheless, it was legible." The teacher agreed.

All students in the class were running and rummaging around like headless chickens. They did not have a clue what to do.

"Who is a Dumbo now!" I said. "By the way, all you need to do is look. All items are stamped with the information you need."

The teacher just kept on reading his book.

I said my piece and goodbye to the class and left. I never returned.

I told my boss I will not go there again; it was just a waste of time.

THE ARROGANT ENGINEER!

Late 1970's

One of the directors, who was an engineer of the company I was working for, bought a second-hand electric fork truck. It cost between £4-5000. When it arrived, we had difficulty removing it from the transporter as it was inoperative (dead as a dodo).

We (factory employees) eventually got it into the workshop and put the battery on charge.

The following day, I check the battery and found it to be in good order. The fork truck was working but very sluggishly, for several days. Maybe 7 to 10 days, but no more.

This particular day the word got around to the managing director that his purchased fork truck was not working. He had his manager, and the other director came to the workshop where I was working. I was within earshot and could see that he was very upset. I had an opportunity to intervene with his conversation between manager and director.

I told them that I could fix this. He arrogantly snarled at me in a loud voice and rejected this out of hand. I backed off quickly and carried on with what I was doing. Several hours passed, and I heard that he's going to get the Coventry climax engineer to have a look at the fork truck.

Sure enough, the engineer turned up mid-morning the next day. He got straight down to business and looked at it. 45 minutes later, he came back to me and said both motors (which are electric) have to be scraped and replaced with new ones.

"Oh, shit!" I thought to myself. "What a nonsense! Motors of this type are heavily insulated and do not burn out."

I took the engineer to the Managing Director's office and left him.

As I left the office block, I bumped into my manager; he asked me what I thought. I told him what the engineer said, they have to be scrapped.

His comment was something like: "I don't think he will like this."

I broke the news to him that he had to pay £200 cash to the engineer for a call out.

"Oh shit! That is insult to injury," he uttered, and walked away.

Later that day, I understood that the two electric motors would cost in the region of £2000 each.

During the day I got a chance to talk to my manager about the dead forklift truck.

I said: "I told you earlier that I could do this job. If you give me Friday, Saturday and Sunday and I can get this fork truck running for you on Monday morning. Is that okay? Give me the three days, with Brian to help."

"Why Brian?"
"I need his strength."

He looked at me and replied: "Are you that confident that you can do this?"

"I am extremely confident."

"Okay, I will talk to both directors and come back to you."
I did not divulge as to why I knew that these motors are not broken. They are just full of shit, sand oil, and grease.

I got the go ahead, and we both made a reasonable amount of money, due to the three-day working week. (That squeezed the household budget hard.)

My boss was a big-headed director, and that's putting it mildly. Yes! I was arrogant too. But I need to convince him to trust me; that I can do what I say I can do.

My manager and I knew that we saved the company thousands of pounds. By the way, the managing director never acknowledged me personally, but I'm sure he got the message yet again about my capabilities.

BIG WHITE ELEPHANT!

Early 1990s

The company I was working for summoned me to the board meeting. I was shocked and bewildered as to why the heck they wanted me at the board meeting. They put me at ease and asked me to sit down. There was a whole lot of waffling, and eventually, I was asked to do a full maintenance schedule for the company. In short, I had no idea of how to do that, so I asked for assistance. They agreed, and a person from Birmingham University was allocated to help me one day every other week.

I guessed that the company knew it had to change the way of doing things, due to E. U. regulations etc. Plus, a new law was introduced to protect from a medical term called "white finger vibration". It was put into law as an industrial injury, and I believe the insurance company told this company that it had to show some kind of program to mitigate any future claim.

This particular injury is caused by extensive vibration to the hands due to badly maintained tools. High-frequency hand tools are extremely efficient, but the downside is, they require regular expensive maintenance, i.e. changing high precision bearings etc to minimise vibration.

Now, my workshop had a blank wall which was perfect for the constructed of the maintenance schedule as the idea was to make it visible to everyone who entered my workshop. It consisted of 2 foot by 4 foot by 8 foot peg boards hung on the wall side-by-side. The top to bottom left side of the board were the days of the year. The top row was for tools and jobs allocated on a regular basis.

Over several months, the progress was slow at first, but eventually it grew into a fully workable schedule. It could be seen and would work very well. The professor from the University of Birmingham told me, "It is now ready to activate". He said he would organise a full board meeting with all relevant people. Eventually, all relevant persons attended the board meeting. The law was laid down more or less by the board that this maintenance schedule must work. A few comments were made by several people. They wanted to know (in short) how this would work? The professor was adamant that this should work very well if everybody cooperated. The board asked me directly if I had anything to say.

I replied bluntly, "You want this to work? I have worked here for 12 plus years and knowing how this company operates, I am not sure it will work! But I'll do my best." With that, I got up and left the boardroom as I had no more to say in this meeting.

The day of reckoning came, and I came in early that morning to make sure that I was up and running. As soon as one manager from his department knew that I was in my workshop, he stormed in and shouted, "I have a problem. Can you please attend to it?"

"NO! I will attend to your problem within 30 minutes."

He screamed at me, "Get your fucking arse to the breakdown right NOW!"

I reminded him that a new system was in operation.

"Now piss off!"

With that, he turned around and slammed the door shut. Within a few minutes or so, my manager stormed in and insisted I drop everything and see to this problem immediately, which I promptly did under protest. Need I say any more? It was business as usual. As from then on, the Fire Fighting (this term used to describe going from one breakdown to the next) continued for another eight years.

GIVING ME INSTRUCTIONS!

Early 1990s

I distinctly remember it was one Friday, early morning. The door to my workshop burst open. The person who entered was the (arrogant) managing director clutching a cardboard box. He immediately described how he tried (without success for several hours' last night) to retrieve the broken parts. The only way was to do the following.

He told me to drill into each broken part, then tap (put a thread in into the hole) and screw a bolt in then pull them out.

He was mumbling about his wife having to cook for the weekend party they were holding and needed this urgently. He would mention this to my manager.

"So could you do that for me?" he asked.

While he was jabbering on about entertainment this weekend, I was thinking about this very simple problem of his.

Somehow, I have no idea how; he managed to break two mixing spatulas flush to the motor casing.

He turned around and went to my manager's office. I promptly cracked opened my vice and taped the body of the mixer on top of vice while holding down the top button of mixer and the broken parts fell out.

I was right behind the managing director as he entered the manager's office clutching the offending parts in my right hand, the managing director was telling the manager (as he walked around the desk) that I was involved in doing an urgent job for his wife as she was entertaining this weekend and needed a hand mixer. The manager looked at me (as I entered) and asked me, "Can you do the job?"

I glanced at the manager with a stern face and immediately focused on the managing director. I slammed my right hand down forcibly on the table in front of his face and looking directly into his eyes and said: " It takes brains to do my job". With nothing more said, I left the manager's office.

A few hours later, the manager came into my workshop and said: What the hell was all that about?" I told him!
Several months back, during the holiday shut down, and I got a mouthful of abuse, telling me that I don't know what I was doing, etc. This is my turn to get back at him for the abuse he gave me, and he knew it. The manager commented that he was speechless for the best part of 2 to 3 minutes. He laughed and said: "What an excellent story!" Then he turned around and left.

The Absurdity of Secrecy

This company was making aluminium bronze castings only for the Admiralty. Usually, the majority of the castings had to be X-rayed to find defects, and this particular casting was also pressure tested.

This casting was in the region of 10 to 12 plus feet long. The circumference in places was 18 to 20 plus inches with several chambers. Weighing 1.5 plus tons, it was part of a nuclear submarine's periscope.

The whole casting was machined, plus riddled with varied sizes of machine-drilled, tapped holes. (A tap is a tool to put a thread into the hole). All holes had to be plugged.

I spent approximately a week testing the plugs with water pressure in the region of 1000 pounds per square inch, and making sure no leaks were found of any kind, internal or external.

Another thing I had to contend with was, of course, ensuring there was no damage to the machine casting while I was tossing, turning and tilting it to remove trapped air.

Six hours was the designated time span for air to be able to seep into another chamber through the porosity of the casting. This would give pressure gauge needle movement, thus indicating a leak.

The day came when the official test was to be carried out by an Admiralty man. Manufacturing casting for the navy, in particular nuclear power submarines, creates anxiety. There is a call for secrecy from the top brass in the home office. Hence, I was instructed by my management to be with him at all times. I collected this gent from the railway station. He was dressed in a pinstriped suit with a bowler hat, umbrella and a leather briefcase (no doubt holding his sandwiches and flask), a book, plus his secret pressure gauge. I was instantly reminded of a radio programme called "The man from the ministry".

Now! Here is the absurdity of all the secrecy. The gauge face is completely blank, apart from a crack in the covering of the gauge allowing you to see the needle when it reached its appropriate pressure. The test was to see if the needle deviated from its position on reaching its desired pressure for six hours. My gauge on the pump was certified by the manufacturing company to Admiralty specification; so was his.

The gent sat down and asked me to proceed with the test. I asked, "what pressures do you want?"

He said, "just put the pressure on."

That I did. A few minutes later, he shouted "Stop!"

His gauge had reached the desired pressure. Mine showed 500lb per square inch. I recalled asking him; "Is that all you want? It is only 500lb per square inch."

He mumbled a few words and carried on reading his book.

Thinking back, he never divulged any figures at all about the pressure test. Six hours later, the test was completed, and he asked me to remove his pressure gauge. He asked me to take him to managers office. On entering the office my manager asked if all was okay,

He replied "Yes!", looking first at the manager, then at me. He said nothing about the test. I said the test went perfectly okay, but he only expressed his thanks for the courtesy given to him and asked for transport back to station. After a day or so, confirmation came through that the test was satisfactory.

Brick versus Prick!

1970s

The foundry environment was very noisy and dusty due to oil burning furnaces and very intense labour. Hence a number of young lads were employed for non-dangerous, laborious duties.

This was the era of Bruce Lee's famous Kung Fu, and his infamous Karate chop. His films were prevalent in the cinema and on television, and a lot of martial arts clubs started up.

Over lunch breaks several lads would mess about, goading and prodding each other, daring one another to do stupid things.
There was a young lad aged 18 to19 amongst the rowdy bunch of lads. He was being heckled and jeered and they were generally making a hell of a noise. 4 to 5 young lads, not much older than him, were trying to persuade him to perform a karate chop on a brick. A normal household brick. This young lad was saying that he could do just that.

I appeared at the point of when one lad goading him to chop the brick in half—but told him to the brick on its side.
I shouted, "Don't be such a bloody Prick!"
There was a lot of shouting and laughing, and at that moment, his right-hand hit the brick at full force.

There was total silence for a few seconds, then a lot of laughing and jeering. This young lad had damaged his right hand, probably for life.

There was not a sound from him, he was just standing there his face was white as a sheet of paper. No blood, but the small finger was right up to where the index finger was, the middle of the hand had a vertical straight edge up to the level of the index finger. One could fit the brick into that part of the hand perfectly. It was not a pretty sight. Of course, the brick is still there, intact and didn't even move.

The manager told a driver to take him to hospital, and that's the last I saw of this lad.

The hospital informed the health and safety executive as a requirement, as it was technically an industrial accident.

A few days later, I saw a man with the manager heading my way armed with an idiot board. I was introduced and told he was from the health and safety executive; the man quizzed me what I knew about this saga then departed.

I heard from the manager a week later that no further action on this matter.

Large Aluminium Extrusion Company

The Five Disciples (Supervisors)

At a large aluminium extrusion company, we had lots of overtime over the weekends. On such a weekend, we started by gathering around table in the canteen. The manager gave a list of jobs to one of the supervisors. My ears pricked up when one of the tasks was given to a co-worker and a supervisor.

I was flabbergasted to learn that this job was to change a cable to a one-ton hoist. Now, there was nothing strange about that in itself, but what was strange was the length of time that was allotted to do the job. They suggested that it would take all morning as it had apparently in the past.

I shouted out, "You've got to be joking? That is a half hour job; no longer than that!"

I placed a bet that I could do it in that time. The whole work force, including supervisors, jumped up and put a bet on with me there and then. One supervisor out of the five held the money.

He asked me if I could cover this amount.

I said, "No need to, as that cash is mine!"

The challenge was on. I took my time, as I knew full well that I could do this. I had been trained by the manufacturer of this hoist.

The designated supervisor and co-worker took two chairs, sat down and watched. I got my tools plus a broom for sweeping the floor. Keeping the cable clean is paramount to assembly. Of course, I also had a ladder.

"You can start timer now," I said.

I completed the job with several minutes spare.

*

Later on that same day, I was called into the supervisors office. Upon entering, I was confronted by five fuming supervisors. I had been anticipating this all day, so I was prepared. All five of them in turn tore the strip off me. The exact wording escapes me, but I do know a lot of swear words were used very loudly. It was clear that they were humiliated and embarrassed. When the verbal onslaught finished, one asked for my response.

"You gave me a bollocking, now I'm telling you this; you all should be ashamed of yourselves! You should never have accepted this challenge in the first place, it shows you how weak, arrogant, and greedy you are. I was glad to have shown the five of you for what you are in front of your work force. Taking this money off you must have hurt!"

It was clear from that day on my days were numbered, but I was very pleased with myself. I had showed all five supervisors up once again, and I made well over £100 cash!

12 Hour Night Shift

Our Maintenance Department would charge other companies to come and maintain their equipment. During a night shift, I came to learn that the main automatic press (the extruding press) at Cheltenham Rubbish Tip was being calibrated frequently. I understood that this process occurred nearly every weekend and involved several lasers.

I voiced my opinion that it was an absurdity to be trying to calibrate with lasers when this heavy machine had been built on top of Cheltenham Rubbish tip.

All my working colleagues, including supervisors, didn't understand or didn't want to know that there was a rubbish tip underneath this huge machine weighing several tons.

It was obvious to me that this was a huge concrete raft, and this building was placed on top of the concrete raft without pile driving it for stabilisation.
They dismissed my comments out of hand.

I thought to myself, "this company was lacking serious brainpower!", but who cared? The Maintenance Department were just fleecing the company.

I cannot recall to whom I said this, but it created quite a stir. I was told not to be so stupid; that I didn't know what I was talking about. I must have used swear words something like: "It is obvious that you fucks don't know either, as one has to stop production for calibration!"

On the same night shift, I had to deal with an Automatic Paint Spraying machine and what a job that turned out to be! This machine was in an enclosure where cellulous paint is being sprayed. This paint would penetrate and congeal the grease, causing the machine to clog up. To make matters worse, this enclosure had no extraction.

I spoke out, saying "why do you not use Molybdenum disulphide lubricant?"
This lubricant is either sprayed onto the chain or dipped then hung up and it would dry very quickly in minutes. It would leave a dry Film, which would not clog the machine up, as nothing would stick to it. My co-worker did not know about this lubricant, and, as it turned out, neither did the supervisors.

He told me that the supervisors had deemed it appropriate to lubricate with grease. I was flabbergasted!

Yes, I did get another verbal drilling from two supervisors...

My Sacking.

"I'm Sorry but I Have to Let You Go"

This happened at midday on a Friday. I was with my co-worker, Ned, and we were discussing things; like how and why they put up with me as nobody had said anything about how I was fitting into the department. I passed a comment that there were too many differences of opinion and conversations with supervisors, who apparently could not make their minds up.

Ironically, a few moments later, the manager entered the workshop at a quick pace, and squeezed straight past us. Not a word or gesture was uttered, but he marched straight to the supervisor's office where he stayed for 10 to 20 minutes. He came out and marched past Ned and me. The manager flung the workshop door open and headed towards his office at a quick pace. It was all very ominous.

"This is it!" I told Ned. I packed my tools into my toolbox and locked it up straight away.

Few minutes passed, then a supervisor (the biggest idiot) came out and told me to follow him to the manager's office.

I looked at Ned and nodded to him, I said quietly, "I'll see you in a minute."

On entering the office, I saw that there were two chairs placed in front of the manager's desk. We both sat down and waited for him to finish fumbling about with paper on his desk. Eventually he looked up, and rather sheepishly told me that he no longer needed my services and would have to let me go.

One or two moments later he asked me if I have any comments. I was glad that he gave me the opportunity to say something.

"Yes! Thank you!" I replied forcefully. "Of course I have, but I don't think you want to hear what I am going to say."

I let him have it with both barrels.

In a forceful voice, I said, "I am surprised that it took you this long to come and tell me that I'm fired. The people you want to fire are all five supervisors. They are the laziest supervisors I have ever met, especially during night shift! Every supervisor on duty enters their den around 23:00, locks the door, switches the lights and radio off and that's the end of it. Nobody hears from them until around five o'clock in the morning. Numerous times, we have no tea or lunch breaks, we have just ploughed straight through, fire fighting for an entire12 hour shift."

The supervisor sitting next to me is the biggest idiot of the five, sitting there, elbows on his knees and face buried in his hands looking down at the floor, he never looked up once.

I continued. "No doubt I'm sticking my neck out, but I don't care! You are involved in fleecing the company by claiming excessive overtime etc. with your five supervisors."

The manager face was a treat to see. He was just dumfounded, open mouthed with wide open eyes and a hint of red appearing on his face. I thought; "he is coming to the boil, time for me to go!"

With that I got up and said "goodbye", then walked out.

I walked up to the workshop, where Ned was, and I told him that I was fired. He did not believe me; he was speechless.

I told Ned, "Don't worry, he got both barrels from me; I told them what I thought of them!"

Then I wished him well and left.

Dysfunctional Company

I joined this company and stayed for 2 months, maybe? I was absolutely blown away by the sheer stupidity. I couldn't how this company could continue to exist. I am certain they had never heard of health and safety rules. A safe working environment did not exist, plus managerial incompetence...

The first job I was called to was to repair a guillotine. You have all heard of corrugated steel sheets, they are everywhere, especially on farms and on industrial building sites. The sizes vary from 6 to 8 feet in length and 2 to 4 foot in width or whatever the customer wants.

Now, here is an example how stupid no! idiotic! things got.

The high tensile cutting blade came loose from the cutting arm, which belonged to a large guillotine. All it needed to fix this was to replace the missing and damaged counter sunk screws (1/2 dozen or so).

I asked the foreman, "where are the screws for securing this blade as this must have happened before?"

He replied, "we have none! You'll have to go and get some."

There was no storeroom of any kind, which I thought strange.

So, I went to the industrial supply outlet just up the road and asked for this type of screw. I showed him the kind I was looking for.

He asked, "what company are you from?"

I told him.

He burst out laughing. "You will be back in half an hour to hand them back!" he said. "Nonsense, just a few pounds worth of screws, that's all," I said.

"It doesn't matter what the cost, the manager will not let you buy them!" he replied.

I said, "Okay, just let me sign for them please?"

I got back, and assembled my tools, including the safety equipment, to make the machine safe to work on. I had just started to remove the damaged screws to begin replacing them with new ones when the manager stopped beside me and bellowed obscenities.

Then he asked the stupid question, "what are you doing?"
I told him that I had purchased screws so I could complete this job quickly, easily and correctly.
Oh shit! GCHQ might as well have been on red alert again!
He gave me more verbal diarrhoea for purchasing screws without his permission. The cost was minimal. I could not understand this stupid individual. What a brain-dead moron he was.

He shouted at me, "Take them back now!"
That I did, in due course.
He told me instead to weld the high tensile steel blade to the guillotine cutting arm.
"You what?" I shouted. I was completely blown away by the stupidity of this idiot.
"You would need special welding rods!" I shouted.
"Nonsense!" was his reply.
I shouted back at him, "you want me to weld this NOW?"
"Yes, now!" was the reply. "Just do it!"
Then he walked away.

I didn't know where all the equipment was, so it took me several minutes to locate everything. Before I started to weld, I told the supervisor and all the men who were standing around:
"It is on your heads what is going to happen next!"
I stitch welded the high tensile steel cutting blade to hold it in place prior to doing a full-blown weld. About two minutes into the welding, the first Ping! was heard, then the second Ping! then the third Ping!

Do you know what happened next? The high tensile steel cutting blade was in 4 or 5 pieces on the floor. The foreman said, "what am I going to do now?"

My words were very simple; "I don't give a shit."

Nothing more was said about this job.

Dysfunctional Company

Part 2.

Fork Truck

This company had a large fork truck, (no manufacture's name). By the look of it, it had been made in the dark ages, had never seen an oil can or grease gun of any description and was generally totally and utterly lacking any maintenance whatsoever. Even the tyres on this fork truck showed signs of metal through the tyre in some places. That's how thin the tyres were; 1 millimetre thick if that!

On this particular day, the manager came round with a brown A4 size envelope telling me that the insurance company had sent some documents regarding the fork truck, and he wanted me to look at it. He handed me the envelope and walked away. It was a certificate of some kind from the insurance company.

On closer inspection, the certificate was a "condemned" notice. I was horrified to see the total number of faults on this fork truck. I sat down and studied this report closely. The report is two years old! And yet, anyone and everyone was driving this fork truck. In my eyes, that was totally criminally insane.

I stopped the driver who was using the fork truck at this time and told him to get off this fork truck as it had been condemned. A few minutes later, a supervisor came and told me he needs the fork truck for about 10 minutes. I gave him the bad news that this fork truck has been condemned for the past two years. He didn't bat an eyelid and couldn't care less. He just got on the fork truck and drove it away. Some time passed he returned with the fork truck and said, "all yours!"

I was stopped umpteen times during my inspection. I was particularly concerned in the lifting chain and hydraulic ram linkages were very loose and worn. The lifting chain was dangerously worn. The tilting linkage was excessively worn. I continued with my inspection on different parts of the fork truck and found many parts just in a bad state and in need of repair or replacing.

Approximately 1 hour before going home, I phoned the tyre specialist up for information on the tyres for the fork truck, which I had zero information about. Shortly after that, I went home.

The next day, the manager came to me looking angrily and said, "why the hell did you get the tyre people in?"
I said, "you are joking, aren't you?"
A stern reply, "No, I'm not!"
I said "Okay, where on this fork truck does this say the tyre size? Please tell me or give me the manual for this fork truck!"
He replied, "there is nothing wrong with the tyres. In future, if you want somebody in, you tell me, and I'll organise it. Is that understood?"

"That's fine by me. By the way, I have estimated the cost of repairs to this fork truck to be somewhere between 10 and £15,000."
He looked at me with a face made out of stone; he just stoned walled me.
I was left in limbo. ZERO, NADA, was said!
I cannot recall what happened next. Nothing more was done to this fork truck as far as I know.

Dysfunctional Company

Part 3.

Safety Guard

The saga continues.

Here is a guillotine combined with a pressing capability without any safety guard. The health and safety inspector gave instructions not to be used until this safety guard has been fitted.

The cost of purchasing all the necessary equipment including lasers and electrical switches etc. is somewhere in the region of £12-£1500.

I shall not bore you with intricate part of building the gadget around this machine. I vaguely recall it took something like 2 to 4 days of putting this together.

I got to work on Monday morning to find that the workforce wanted blood. The main reason was that the manual workforce was sent home on Saturday morning (no overtime pay) as this machine was unable to be operated by the workforce. World War three was in full swing!

The manager was fuming! The supervisor was fuming and yelling at me!

"How the f*cking hell can we work without putting our hands near the cutting blade and press?"

The manager shouted at me to remove it immediately. I point-blank refused to do so and ignored him. This was a safety device to stop people from getting injured.

"Show me what you are doing please." I said.

The workforce showed me what they had to do.

My reaction was, "That's fine, but you need to change your working practice by placing the sheet where you want to cut or bend it, and then moving your hands away."

Again, the manager shouted at me to remove the f*cking frame. I point-blank refused to remove anything unless I receive a signed piece of paper from The Managing Director.

I did get that, (eventually), so I removed the whole safety guard and placed it in a heap next to the machine.

That is it.

Paper and pencil = 0!

Part 4

The stupidity never stopped! Next job was to fix the lighting in this factory. I was instructed to find all the faults and rectify and replace all the lighting. Before I could do that, I would have to cost it first.

I knocked on the locked office door, whereupon a young girl opened the door and said "yes?"

"I need a pencil and paper please."

"NO!" was the reply.

"What? Why the hell not?"

"You need the manager's permission for that!"

My reply was "don't be so f*cking stupid, it's just paper-and-pencil."

The answer was still "NO".

Eventually I found the idiot and he gave me a written slip with his signature on it, I said, "it is totally ridiculous the way you run this place!"

I received zero response.

Yes! Eventually, I did get one sheet of paper and pencil.

I spent one complete day, up and down the ladder testing this and that. The next day, I asked for permission to go to the local electrical store to look at pricing. My request was granted. I returned with all the relevant information and handed it to the manager.

He looked at the paper for a minute folded up and tore it up.

I shouted " what the hell did you do that for? I have spent all this time going up and down a bloody ladder and you just ripped it up!"

His words were, "I'm not spending that kind of money." (The figure was less than £1000).

I left soon after this. I don't think one job was completed, in the time I was with the company.

Being Unemployed

I was then unemployed for several months, this meant having to do the daily task of looking for a job. That meant walking 3 miles into the job centre and back. I was supposed to log down what I was looking at, but I never did this as no interviewer ever asked to see this. Several months passed with this daily quest.

After waiting 12 months, I received an appointment from the hospital for a minor operation to remove a small fragment of steel lodged deep inside my left wrist. This meant having to sign off the unemployment register and sign onto sickness benefit. Several weeks later I had to do all of this in reverse. This turned out to be a little trickier.

The day came to do this, so I made my way upstairs to the relevant department. It was being run by civil servants who have no sense of compassion, just a straight face and dogmatic attitude.

I asked the lady at the desk for the appropriate form to sign back in after being off sick. I made an appointment with her that same day at 14:00 hours.

A huge number of questions on the form were not applicable, so I filled the blank spaces with N/A.

The allotted time arrived, and I entered the room. There at the far end of the room, dead ahead, sat this lady, who was 50 to 60 years of age. She was behind her large desk filled with papers, an electronic typewriter, a phone etc. On the right side, against the wall, were three chaps with stone-faced expressions sitting 6 feet apart from each other behind their desks. This reminded me of the three monkeys (see no evil, speak no evil, hear no evil). The rest of the room was totally empty apart of couple of chairs.

I handed the form to the lady, she glanced at the first page and immediately said, "you have not filled the form in properly". My response was very simple and forthright yet polite "Yes, I have." She refused point blank to look at any more pages of the form. (Now my blood pressure was building up).

I said in an agitated yet forceful voice, "if you let me see one of the gents over there I will do as he tells me, and I will apologise."
The reply was emphatic, "NO. You'll see NO one."

I glanced at the three monkeys behind their desks. Zero reactions from them. I was seeing RED at this time; my blood pressure was getting higher by the second. I slipped into a rage and fury without thinking. I snatched the form from the desk, tore it to pieces, then bent over the desk, and threw the pieces at her, aiming for her cleavage. She immediately set off the "panic alarm", and as I turned round, I glanced at the three monkeys. They could have been cardboard; not a movement of any kind. Then I left the room.

On reaching the stairs, I met two security guards running up the stairs. I told them there was a woman having conniptions. I just kept on walking downstairs and out of the building. That was that. I did not return until 15 years or so later. Next day I went to an employment agency. Yes! they did write to me; I totally ignored the letters.

Cold Store

RED FACED LUNATIC

I was contracted out by an employment agency in Cheltenham. This agency had a large range of companies on their book's that required short term contracts. In a short time, the lady who was running this agency came to know my capabilities. I could put my hand to most jobs.

One day towards the end of a week she phoned me and offered me this job that would start on Monday. They were desperate to have a person who is reliable.

I happened to visit my brother that weekend and mentioned that I had a job starting on Monday, not far away from where he lives, in a Cold store.

He burst out laughing and said "Pablo! You're not going to stay at that job for long. He's a lunatic"

I said, "we'll see about that."

At nine o'clock in the morning I arrived at the company and asked to see this chap. I was told you'll find him in the huge cold store. On entering, it felt chilly I guess 5°C or so. Sure enough, he was at the centre of this huge industrial building.

This was a logistics hub for all meat products going to supermarkets. There were lots of trolleys bearing white boxes with huge 10 plus digits stamped on top. The dimensions of these boxes are approximately 18 inches long by 9 to 10 inches high by 12 inches wide. Around the walls and 10 to 15 feet off the floor, boards were hanging with large 10 plus digits printed on them. Underneath each one of these numbered boards was a large movable trolley on a pallet that would be moved by fork truck when full, then replaced with an empty one. I would estimate approximately hundred or so trollies were in this huge cold store.

I made my way to the centre of this cold store and introduced myself, with no effect. The man was shouting and yelling at the workforce. This individual was about 5 foot 8 inches tall stout. I distinctly recall the colour of his face red, yes bright red and ready to explode. He was extremely agitated or frustrated and couldn't stand still, moving back and forth turning around constantly.

Eventually he looked at me and said in a loud voice "you are from the agency."
I replied "yes, indeed."
"Good!"
He eventually shouted and waved his arm at a young lad to come over. This lad looked frightened and was not used to being shouted at. He was sweating profusely, even in this cold store. He was pushing his trolley full of cardboard boxes stacked nice and tidy in his trolley. This trolley is 6-foot-tall wire mesh sides by 4 foot wide by 6 foot deep one side was totally open.
"Now!" the manager shouted to the boy, "show him and tell him what needs to be done. Off you go!"
I followed this lad here, there and everywhere. He was going back and forth, and I could not understand why? It seemed totally illogical. Each box had a number, which had to go into a container with the corresponding number hanging above it. But the numbers were completely random, so it seemed totally illogical. Why oh why were these numbers not put in consecutive order?

This lad had to push this trolley up and down dodging everybody else's trolley to find the appropriate number. I cannot recollect how many workers are doing this, but there must be about 5 to 10 of them. It was extremely dangerous as two fork trucks were whizzing about in this absolute chaos.

It was my turn to get one of these trolleys and off I went in a confusion, trying to find the numbers. I eventually emptied my trolley except for one box. This box had a number which I could not match up with a container. I headed to the centre where the bright red Balloon was bobbing up and down shouting and yelling.

I got his attention by shouting, "excuse me sir!"
He looked at me and shouted, "Yes?"
I replied, "I'm sorry, but I cannot locate this number anywhere?"

Instead of helping me, he went into orbit, just like letting go of a large inflated red balloon and watching it go in all directions. He was totally wacko. His voice was at full throttle, blasting obscenities at me. Even some words which I don't think I've ever heard! I was seeing red and stopped him dead in its tracks.

I shouted at full throttle, "Who do you think you are shouting at, you heap of shit? Here's your box and shove it up yours."
I turned around and walked away.
He shouted at me, "get back here!"

I cannot recall exactly what I said, but I made it absolutely clear that there was no way I would turn around!

Tea lady

I received a phone call from the agency I was working for one Friday late afternoon. The lady on the phone pleaded with me to become a tea-lady for the week, as the Borough Council tea-lady was called home due to a bereavement.

"Me?" I shouted, "a tea-lady? You've got to be joking!"

She spoke in a stern voice and said, "Please! We are struggling to fill the vacancy this late in the day. I know you can put your hand to anything!"
Hence, I became a tea-lady for the week.

Early on Monday morning, I reported to the council whereupon they showed me where to go and what to do. This chap gave me full instructions and the timetable for the week on an idiot board. Monday to Wednesday early morning was plain sailing.

Around 10 o'clock on Wednesday, I sat down and started my cup of tea, only to be interrupted by a knock on the door. A lady's head poked around the door and said in a high-pitched voice; "Can we have tea please?"

I said, "who are we?"
"The W.I.," was the reply.
I looked at my idiot board for today and found nothing.
My reply was simple, "NOPE!"
The squeaky voice replied, "We always have it on Wednesday!"
"Not this Wednesday," I replied. The head disappeared, and the door slammed shut.

Few minutes passed and the gent came in and asked if there was a problem?

"NO," I said, "do you have a problem? I have my instructions in front of me. simple." I continued sipping my tea.

He asked me if I could supply the W.I. with tea.

"Of course, I can," I said, and with that he disappeared.

In due course, I supplied them with tea. As I entered, pushing the trolley full of tea and teacups one lady shouted out, "where are the biscuits? We usually have half a tin of biscuits!"

"Definitely not! The ratepayers pay for biscuits for the councillors and not for the W.I.!"

I hastened to add; "I do have a large plastic bag full of broken biscuits and I shall get them for you!"

Local Engineering Company

Conundrum

Part 1

This local engineering company wanted an urgent job done. Early that morning, I got to see the manager (very amenable individual). As we walked to this room, he told me that this was an important job. He told me that this had to be done by one person, and that will take up three days to do it. He pointed to the trolley. It was approximately 4 foot long, 3 foot wide and 4 foot high. It had 4 trays full of threaded Allen cap bolts (another name hexagonal head cap bolts) lined up side-by-side. Their size was approximately 4 inches long by about 1 inch in diameter. They had to be coated with some white powder. Why? I cannot recall.

I have been wracking my brain, trying to recall what their usual process was. It must be a very simple job otherwise I would have remembered.

A few minutes into this job, I found it very laborious and long-winded. I decided to experiment with another way. Yes, I found a quicker way that worked well. I finished this job in 6 hours.

Now I had to find the manager. He was nowhere to be seen. Instead, I was told that an inspector was at hand to okay the jobs.

I found this inspector sitting on a highchair against the wall, reading.

Now! If you have ever seen an old 1960s Pipe tobacco tin called "Players Navy Cut", there was an image of a sailor with a black cap, and beard on the lid. Here he was alive! I introduced myself as an agency worker and asked him to see if the job has been completed to his satisfaction.

"What job?" he asked.

I replied, "The job of putting the white coating onto the bolts".

In a voice of disbelief, he said, " you cannot have finished that job?"

"Well! All I want is for you to give me the okay for this job, that's all I ask."

As we walked into the room, he promptly inspected several on the top tray and on 2nd, 3rd, and 4th tray. "How the hell did you manage to do this job so quickly?" he said, in a loud voice of amazement.

My response was, "that doesn't matter. Have you have passed them?"

"Yes," he replied.

"Excellent!" I said.

The Manager was informed in due course.

About an hour or two spent messing about and looking at the machinery etc. This company was producing a lot of items for the railway industry, I found it very interesting but puzzling as to why that job would take 3 days. Very strange.

Eventually, the manager found me and headed towards me with a bounce in his step. He had a huge Cheshire cat smile on his face and looked extremely happy. He thanked me and wanted to know how I was able to do this job so quickly?

"No need to thank me," I said. "All I had to do was to do the job you asked me to do. That's what I've done. Can I go now?"

The manager smiled (no, more of a laugh) at me and said "Not so fast! We've got you for three days! There is another job you can do for us."

"Oh! what is it?" I asked.

"Take accurate measurements of internal tubes, that have been highly polished."

This turned out to be 200 cylinders, approximately 12 inches long, with an internal dimension of 6 inches. One end had a closed dome shaped. This was part of an automatic braking system for marshalling wagons on the railway.

The manager supplied me with some digital internal callipers and one engineering V block, an idiot board and paper and pencil.

He moved rubble off a wooden tabletop and said," here you are!"

I said "I don't think so! You want me to do the measurements with this equipment? The measurements you want are in microns! I need another engineering V block and engineering tabletop to have stability and accuracy."

All this time, the inspector was with the manager. He was listening to what was going on and agreed with me that I need these tools. The manager was bewildered and taken aback. He said; "we have done this job like this before, with only one V block and on this wooden table."

I butted in and said, "you must have had many inconsistent readings. You used wood and steel surfaces; that's a recipe for inaccurate readings, especially with reading microns!"

Eventually this was supplied, and the job started.

Halfway through the last day, (I had about 3 to 4 cylinders to go), I was interrupted by a stranger who wanted to know if I was Pablo.

"Who wants to know?" I replied, in a cagy sort of voice.

He introduced himself Bob or Rob. He said that he was from upstairs.

"So what?" I asked.

"Can you come upstairs with me?"

" No! Defiantly not," I said. "I am employed here to do a job."

His response made it clear that he was from the same company I was working for.

"Okay!" I said, "give me about an hour or so, then come back down and see if I'm finished."

"Okay," he said, and off he went. I thought "strange individual!"

This individual was responsible for my new job.

I Don't Tick the Boxes

Part 2

As I followed that strange individual upstairs, he asked me a lot of questions. What kind of work I did in the past? I gave a brief account; watch repairing, electrical work, hydraulics etc. We reached the room, which was very clean. In this big room, the processes and assembly were carried out. It was completely surrounded in glass and covered to make it completely dustproof. All of the workers were in white gowns or coats.

Now this chap kept talking as I was watched the process. All of the employees were at a different part in the process, and that was far more interesting than having to listen to some kind of verbal diarrhoea about nothing and everything, so I didn't take much notice of it.

Eventually he showed me what exactly needed to be done.

He asked me; "can you do this type of work?"

I replied "Yes, it's very easy. No problem!"

Both of us entered into his office and he started to talk about what is happening imminently to this department, (which is making industrial hydraulic valves). It had been taken over by a huge American company.

We moved downstairs and he told me to come in at eight o'clock on Monday morning. I thanked him for showing me around and declined to do exactly as instructed. I was employed by the agency and could not do that. He insisted that he would deal with this, and I should come in on Monday morning.

He said, "I will arrange all the paperwork for you to hand over to the office on Monday morning before you leave here."

"Okay," I said, "I'll see you."

Later that afternoon, no paperwork was handed to me, and it was time to leave the company. I said farewell to the manager and left minus the paperwork.

On Monday, I decided to turn up at the office as instructed last Friday and asked to see manager from the hydraulics department. The lady at the reception asked for the paperwork. I told the story and she said "Sorry, you can't come in."

"Can't you phone him?"

"No!"

"Okay!" and I about-turned and walked away. As I was doing so, I heard my name being shouted out. I turned around and saw this manager giving hell to the lady. She was supposed to have contacted the Head of HR and he wanted to know why the paperwork had not been supplied to me on Friday? That is another story.

It was a very strange situation, being employed by a company without giving a clocking in card, without any paperwork. I was just told to sit down next to a chap and that he would tell me what to do for this job. This went on for a number of weeks; I was just turning up without clocking in or out.

I cannot recall when this happened, but a chap from Tewkesbury turned up. I cannot recall his name, but he was the Head of HR. He welcomed me to this company and gave me an application form to fill in. He said that in due course, he would come back and pick it up. True to his word, he did come back a few days later to pick the application form up. Well, I thought that was it. A week or so later, I moved up to Tewkesbury and settled down in my new workplace.

One day I was called to HR. It was situated in the middle of a huge open plan office. There were around 100 plus employees, but in this department, I found only 5 to 6 females with a small cubical that was surrounded by frosted glass.

I said my name, and all looked up in astonishment. They had obviously never heard my name.

"I understand someone wants to see me?" I said. One of them pointed to the cubical.

I knocked on the door (it was ajar) and walked in. Here was this chap, I would say middle aged. He asked me to close door and take a chair.

He was baffled by the answers (or lack of) I gave on this application form. The majority of questions were empty, and he wanted to know why? He started by asking me questions, such as where and when I was born, educated, grades, degree, nationalities of parents etc. My answers would complicate matters. There was no way to verify my answers!

For example, I was born 1945 on a Spanish document, (self-administrated) but having English parentages meant that the British Consulate did not register my birth until 1952. After 15 minutes, if not 20 maybe, he was muttering to himself. Eventually he said to me, "I'll have to make another form up for your file."

He shook my hand and said, "you can go now."

I gave a chuckle and left. I was amazed that he didn't even know the capital city of (Paraguay) the country where I was born.

THE PRAT

Philosophy, Responsibility, Accountability, Traceability

(All Out of the Window!)

I was working for this global company here in the UK. At the time, it was mainly servicing and supplying valves for the aircraft industry. The industrial side of things, such as robotic hydraulic valves, was in its infancy. To advance the industrial side, this global company purchased the local company that I had joined recently. That company made hydraulic valves which were not suitable for the aircraft industry.

Between the 1950s to the 80s a number of aircraft crashes worldwide were on the news. This company, being a significant global player in supplying servo valves to this industry, did not want a tarnished reputation. Neither did that want to be found wanting; they didn't want their existing documentation to be out of pace with the rest of the globe industry. Hence the decision to introduce relevant documentation to the whole industrial division.

This policy was implemented to make everybody responsible, accountable and furthermore traceable, if for any reason it was deemed necessary. This was signed by directors, plant managers, managers, supervisors and of course by me. A stamp to be used on each stage of assembly and testing, to signify who done the relevant process.

This policy was quite clear and non-ambiguous. No work or assembly of any kind was to be carried out without accompanying documentation.

This company had a Philosophy that went hand in hand with the above policy; it was outlined in a meeting, that was compulsory to attend. No exclusions. From Managing director to the janitor, all have to attend. I managed to avoid this. Why? This could be another story.

This story is about what happened a few weeks prior of actually leaving.

The years tallied up to 13. Being content, I had no ambition whatsoever. I just wanted to tread water up to my retirement, hoping it would be 60 years. (It, in fact, turned out to be 63).

There was this obnoxious, self-opinionated individual who was very good at organising activities: football, cricket, swimming, events, and tennis plus horse racing, but not very good at anything else. In my opinion, he was just pissing about and not doing what he supposed to be doing. Lazy, downright arrogant, but yet clever enough to stick like chewing gum to his manager.

He was supposed to fill in some of the paperwork for a type of valve with all relevant data, that included nozzles pushing pressures etc. He called himself an associated engineer (whatever that meant). As the years progressed, company policies had changed and amended, but not the one that my story is about.

One day this self-opinionated individual, who was responsible to produce all relevant paperwork, turned up at my workbench unannounced and promptly sat down beside me. This instantly got me agitated and I asked him "what the hell are you doing here?"

His response was, "I've got to do the paperwork for the valve you are assembling and testing."

"To hell you are!" I got up to get a cup of coffee, (no it was drinking chocolate, it tasted better than the coffee), but in reality, I was trying to get away. The coffee station was located in the canteen quite a reasonable distance away. 5 to 10 minutes later I came back to my station, hoping he was gone. Hell! There he was, still waiting for me. I politely said, "please go away, I don't want you here." I was getting more agitated by the second.

My fuse is going into melt down as I sat down. Zero action from him.

"That's it!" I shouted full blast, "will you fuck off?"

I said it without thinking about the consequences.

At this particular time, I was working outside the clean room area. This was an open plan workshop, where everybody could see everybody else. Within no time at all, a whole lot of Bods swarmed around after hearing my loud comment. They wanted to know what the problem was.

I shouted "he doesn't want to go; I can't stand this obnoxious individual. Get him away from me!"

I recall one individual; he was a manager of some department started to tell me off about swearing etc. I cannot recall the exact words I used, but a few swear words were defiantly in use. I was red and hot under my collar. I was extremely angry, agitated and ready to jack this job in with a bang. One of the managers took charge and calmed me down. He wanted an explanation. In a loud voice, so everybody could hear, I said; "This individual has had years and years to sort this paperwork out, and never got to do anything of the sort! In my eyes, he's just pissing about as usual. Numerous times, I have brought this to the attention of supervisors and manager. Nothing has ever happened!"

The seconds flew by. I thought quickly, things are getting out of hand, I was losing the argument. I had to come up with something.

YES, GOT IT!

I leant over to my right and pulled open the bottom draw and retrieved the stamp-dated Policy which all of them signed and slapped this on top of the cabinet. A few seconds passed, like a puff of smoke. As quickly as they came, they diapered one by one.

Noone saw this coming!

My rant was justified, nevertheless. My immediate manager told me afterwards that I was a bastard, and he didn't appreciate me pulling out this policy.

I just smiled at him. I never saw that Prat again.

Trouble Shooting

I was working in assembling and testing industrial servo-valves. The company had quite a few unresolved issues. The management decided to form a troubleshooting team. My immediate manager asked me if I would like to join the team.

"Certainly," I said.

A few days later, the manager that was running this team approached me and wanted to know if I had any problems. I replied, "certainly I have!"

"Good," he said. "Bring it along on Thursday."

On Thursday, I entered a large conference room and found a number of people already there. I was the last to enter. As I sat down, they all introduced themselves. The chairperson asked me by name to start with my problem. That took me by surprise.

The first thing I gave was the valve reference number, and before I could say " Jack Robinson", the chairperson butted in and said "I know this Valve. I have worked with it for 15 plus years."

I was amazed and said, "you do?".

"Certainly!" chairperson said, "before you start talking about your problem, we cannot touch or alter any part of this valve ".

"But…we do!" was my reply.

I was assembling and testing this valve for a number of years and repeatedly questioned as to why I had to use a file to enlarge the holes so the shipping bolts could fit. This meant damage to each unit prior to dispatch. I questioned this repeatedly and told "that is how it is". "Just stupid!" was my thinking! One doesn't simply sell an item to a customer and say, "oh by the way, we damaged the unit on purpose as the bolts don't fit!". Lunacy in the first order.

The chairperson asked the engineer if he had any comments.

"Actually, I am going to the U.S. on Monday on a different matter. I will talk to the responsible department about this valve and report back at the next meeting."

Three or four weeks later we had another meeting. The engineer reported that this valve should have never been sent over to the UK.

"It is a U.S. product only."

I burst out laughing.

"You are telling me that we have been building this valve for decades and not one person in the U.S. twigged this? I cannot believe this!"

The logistical cost would be huge to ship all parts in and then the finished valves back. Lunacy in the 2nd order. Not one person in the room uttered a word of disbelief or gave any emotion. WHY? Brainwashed.

Clean Room Antics

I was working with a female of my age in a clean room on industrial valves. All the others were working on Formula One racing car valves. One of the girls who fancies herself being a manager. In fact, she was just basically a spokesperson for the clean room. One day, I came in from lunch and walked into the clean room to find 3 of them gassing as usual. I got to my workstation to start my job. She! Little Mussolini, marched round the work bench bent over to my right ear and told me: "we start at quarter past not at 25 minutes past the hour, understand?"

I did object to being told off! I was the only one working at this time. I thought about this while I was working and thought, "this is not on! As I am the only male in the clean room, Little Mussolini is taking the piss!" She knew that this rule for tea and lunch breaks was extremely lax.

Best part of half an hour plus, the gassing and giggling continued like nothing ever happened. Well, I carried on working for a short time. I thought; here I am clocking on 60 years of age Little Mussolini in early or mid-twenties! HELL! I am not having this.

I got up and went to the manager's office. It was located in plain view of the clean room and I walked in (his door is always open). He looked at me and saw that I was agitated. I asked him to look at the clean room and tell me: "how many people can you see standing gassing and giggling?"

"3," was the reply.

" Good!" I explained the whole situation. I made it quite clear if he didn't deal with this, I would go to HR. I would not put up with this sort of bullshit.

I looked at him. He acknowledged me by saying, "I will deal with this."

I thanked him and walked back to my workstation.

About an hour or so later, the air lock door flew open, and a loud voice shouted, "Everybody Stop!"

There she stood Red Faced Little Mussolini. She looked straight at me! Her face bright red was like a shining beacon placed on a white smock. Her hands were trembling. She said in a loud shaking voice, "I would like to apologise to you!"

I thanked her and said, "now forget it!" and smiled. She never bothered me again.

Several months later, another incident occurred but with a younger girl and this time no other one of any authority was in the mix. Only a senior executive. Yes, far stronger and colourful language was used. I am sure you can use your imagination.

Monthly Meeting

Gobbledygook

The company decided to inform everybody on the same day what was going on in the company, rather than having meetings arranged hap-hazard by all departments.

This sounded good! But in reality, it was a waste of time as there was a huge variety of different departments and processing going on in this company.

On this day, the manager from the office took the meeting and read to everybody on the shop floor (excluding office staff) from a A4 sheet paper.

After a few minutes of listening to what he had to say, I realised that it was totally incomprehensible and full of abbreviations and references, including numbers which made no sense to me. I shouted across the room "excuse me? Please can you give me some idea of what you are talking about?"

A number of workers shouted out, "just go with the flow".

In a loud voice and to emphasis my outburst, I quickly said, "I bet not one person here can relate to what you're talking about! It's just gobbledygook of the first order!"

Oh, dear me, my outburst and comment were not appreciated.

"If you want to know the relevant information, you can come to my office and I'll be glad to inform you, but not in this meeting!" was the Manager's response. I sensed he was slightly miffed.

Just to let you know, this meeting to give me clarity never materialised, as I'm damn certain he didn't know himself what all this gobbledygook about. A similar thing went on every month.

I tried on several occasions to avoid this meeting by going to canteen or the toilets and waiting a few minutes hoping the manager would not notice. Then I could just slip to my workstation. That did not work either. Someone was called upon to bring me into this meeting. Yes! I was miffed.

Several years passed, and I visited my previous department. It happened to be a Thursday and low and behold, this meeting was about to be held. Yes! I was welcomed in by the manager; there were old and new faces. I greeted them all with something like this; "Good morning! Not more of this nonsense!"

I did notice that he had more sheets of paper (with gobbledygook on no doubt). I cannot recall saying anything but must have done as there was a lot of laughing, I recall seeing a smile from my old manager.

Self-Assessment

A tool was introduced for management to divide and conquer the workforce, not to learn by it. No doubt people will try now, as they have tried in the past, to convince me otherwise. This is my account of the annual saga that my manager inflicted on me. He came in and handed out a comprehensive form, 2 pages double-sided A4 to fill-in. The manager and I had a well-rehearsed routine.

He hands me this form with a smile. I took it and directed it straight to the bin, which was between him and me. He knew the well-oiled saga.

As I ventured out to different departments during the week and bantered with others on this particular subject. Not one person agreed with me that this is a load of nonsense. I have asked myself repeatedly "why is this?"

Here is an example of what happened. In the same building where my workstation is, a lone engineer whose workstation is in a separate room spent the entire working day talking to his manager about the form, just amazing! I found that this form is treated with total reverence, must be guarded, and kept secret by all I came across. I just could not understand this, but I wondered if somehow, I was at fault, for not fitting into this ethos.

The manager came into the clean room and beckoned me to go with him upstairs to where the dedicated office was set up for assessment.
As I followed him into the office I told him forcefully. "You know full well that I have not filled in this form. You can fill in

your form and I'll sign it. In fact, give me your pen and I do it now."

His reply was simple "I have 10 minutes minimum for each person."

I said in an abrupt tone. "I don't care!" I just picked-up his ballpen, took the form that was on table, signed it and pushed it to him. I smiled at him he shook his head and smiled as I walked out of the office. That took no more than 30 seconds.

Many managers (over my working life) could not deal with my frank forthright talking, as I would not conform to their work ethics.

I have my own "ethics" and try to stick to them. When one accepts the employment, one is offered; one does it to the best to one's ability. The manager (if he is any good) should acknowledge this at the appropriate time.

There is a lot of discord in the work force; they constantly wanted more money. My manager encouraged me to apply for a high position many times over the years, but I rejected this idea. Why? The monetary increase was minimal, and the workload was not to my liking. Money is not my driving force, as with most people.

I was dumbfounded to find all my work colleagues spent most of the week talking about how good they are. What a load of bollocks!

The Philosophy Event I Vowed Not to Attend.

I cannot recall how many years or even a decade passed having successfully avoided this event. A lot of bantering about this subject with many different people was to be had. It was clear that there was something amiss. As far as I can recall I was the only employee who was transferred from the buy-out to this company who had not had an invite.

As I stated previously, I was often employed through the back door, having never filled in the standard application form issued by the company prior to employment.

The Head of HR, (nickname "I'll get back to you"—which he seldom did) probably forgot all about me, my file, or my application form. All very plausible, plus dare I say, he was old and incompetent. All contributing factors.

OR! The new head of HR had only just found my file. Those are the only explanations I can come up with. I was told in so many words about these meetings repeatedly over the years. My manager kept saying "It is one of the compulsory things you have to attend in this company. Every individual must go to this meeting without exceptions."

I was very dogmatic and bullish, saying "I will never attend this!"

My manager said, "you will have to attend eventually!"

I just shook my head and said, "no way!"

The time eventually came when a member from HR department presented me with a beautifully embossed envelope. I opened it, low and behold there was a letter inviting me to attend the prestigious event. The letter was shortly followed by a visit from my manager. He came purposely to see me, a broad smile on his face.

"I told you so! You will not be missed! You have your invitation!"

I was in a quandary, not knowing what to say or do. I repeated to myself hundreds of times in my head; "must find a way not to attend!" It was bothering me for the rest of that day, and following days. I just cannot tell a direct lie as that is too final and really not me. I needed a solid gold cover story that would be plausible, binding and totally safe and cannot be checked.

What I wrote is not a direct lie, but a distorted, maybe twisted, yes even stretched version of the truth. I really was suffering from dizzy spells at that time and my work colleagues knew of this (that's the truth).

To get me out of attending this prestigious event, here was the answer. I spun a yarn (grant you a long one) about my blood pressure. The anxiety of being out of my comfort zone would increase my blood pressure, and the doctor did tell me not to get stressed in so many words.

I typed my story and delivered it to HR. Some time passed I received a very sympathetic reply excusing me from attending this prestigious event. I was really chuffed with this.

My manager was duly notified that I was excused and that annoyed him. He was round like a shot to see me. In a stern, loud voice, he wanted to know how I got excused.

I said, "On medical grounds."

"Bullshit!" was his reply.

Supporting very talented local, independent,
and self-published authors.

Thank you for supporting us.

All our books are available at

www.honesty-press.sumupstore.com

355f1dba-fc5a-40bc-bbe9-5611a76a4e8fR06